RESEAR[
CONTR

☐ **Yes,** I want the Rese ... to fund inno-vative research that advances the investment management profession. Please accept my tax-deductible contribution at the following level:

☐ Contributing Research Fellow . . . .$25,000 to $49,999
☐ Research Fellow . . . .$10,000 to $24,999
☐ Contributing Donor . . . .$1,000 to $9,999
☐ Donor . . . .$100 to $999
☐ Friend . . . .$ ________

☐ My check is enclosed (payable to the Research Foundation of AIMR).
☐ I would like to donate appreciated securities (send me information).
☐ Please charge my donation of $ ____________ to my credit card.
☐ VISA ☐ MC ☐ Amex ☐ Diners ☐ Corporate ☐ Personal

Card Number

____/____
Expiration Date

Name on card PLEASE PRINT

☐ Corporate Card
☐ Personal Card

Signature

☐ This is a pledge. Please bill me for my donation of $____________.

☐ I would like recognition of my donation to be:
☐ Individual donation ☐ Corporate donation ☐ Different individual

PLEASE PRINT NAME OR COMPANY NAME AS YOU WOULD LIKE IT TO APPEAR

PLEASE PRINT ☐ Mr. ☐ Mrs. ☐ Ms. MEMBER NUMBER ____________

Last Name (Family Name) First Middle Initial

Title

Address

City State/Province Country ZIP/Postal Code

4JAC

Please mail this completed form with your contribution to:
Research Foundation • P.O. Box 3668
Charlottesville, VA 22903-0668 USA

For more on the Research Foundation of AIMR, please visit www.aimr.org and select the Research Foundation under "Featured Areas".

Tell Us Your Research Needs

The Research Foundation's mission is to encourage education for investment practitioners worldwide and to fund, publish, and distribute relevant research. The Foundation emphasizes research of practical value to investment professionals while exploring new and challenging topics that provide a unique perspective in the rapidly evolving profession of investment management.

These are just a few of the topics under consideration by the Research Foundation Review Board:

- ☐ Global sectors
- ☐ Risk management
- ☐ Asset allocation
- ☐ Asset and liability management
- ☐ Volatility
- ☐ Hedge funds

Please check which of these research topics you would like to see, or suggest your own topics below. Our goal is to provide research that helps you to perform your investment management duties better and to maintain your competitive edge while ultimately better serving your clients. We will offer your thoughts at an upcoming meeting of the Research Committee.

TOPIC ____________________

TOPIC ____________________

TOPIC ____________________

We thank you for your ideas.

Visit www.aimrpubs.org for the latest investment research.

Jens Carsten Jackwerth
University of Konstanz
Germany

Option-Implied Risk-Neutral Distributions and Risk Aversion

The Research Foundation of AIMR™

ISBN 0-943205-66-2

Printed in the United States of America

March 31, 2004

Editorial Staff
Elizabeth A. Collins
Book Editor

Sophia E. Battaglia
Assistant Editor

Kara H. Morris
Production Manager

Lois A. Carrier/Jesse Kochis
Composition and Production

Mission

The Research Foundation's mission is to encourage education for investment practitioners worldwide and to fund, publish, and distribute relevant research.

Biography

Jens Carsten Jackwerth is a professor of economics at the University of Konstanz, Germany. He was a visiting postdoctoral scholar at the University of California at Berkeley until 1997 and taught at the London Business School until 1999 and then at the University of Wisconsin at Madison before taking his current position in 2001. His research interests are derivatives pricing and asset pricing—in particular, how to unlock the information contained in option prices to gain insight into the underlying probabilities and beliefs held by market participants. In related research, Professor Jackwerth has investigated stochastic processes for stock prices that are consistent with observed option prices. His work has appeared in the *Journal of Finance, Review of Financial Studies, Journal of Portfolio Management*, and *Journal of Derivatives*. Professor Jackwerth received his PhD in finance from Göttingen University in 1994.

Contents

Foreword

The development of option-pricing theory is perhaps the most significant achievement in financial economics, if not all of economics. Moreover, it has a wonderfully rich history, parts of which are recounted here. Long before Fischer Black and Myron Scholes and Robert Merton nailed it, luminaries such as the French mathematician Louis Bachelier, the brilliant economist Paul A. Samuelson, and the famous card counter Ed Thorp contributed to the ultimate solution. And let's not forget Albert Einstein, whose unwitting contribution to option-pricing theory through his exploration of Brownian motion was cited as one of the key contributions that led to his Nobel Prize in physics.

Option-pricing theory is significant not only for the intellectual advances it inspired, however, but also because it contributes to social amenity—perhaps more so than some of the more obvious and heralded achievements in the natural sciences. Options afford producers and service providers a mechanism to hedge risk, which allows them to offer their products and services at lower prices than they would otherwise require. A robust option-pricing framework facilitates these hedging activities and, therefore, promotes broad access to critical goods and services.

Finally, option-pricing theory offers a prism by which valuable information about expectations and risk preferences is revealed to us, which is the topic of this fine Research Foundation monograph by Jens Carsten Jackwerth. Investors have long used option prices to infer market expectations about the volatilities and correlations of the underlying assets. After the stock market crashed in 1987, investors and researchers noticed that the volatilities implied by option prices on the same underlying asset differed depending on the strike prices of the option contracts. The initial approach for reconciling these differences was to depart from the standard assumption that returns are lognormally distributed and, instead, infer the distribution that would give rise to these differences in implied volatilities. A subsequent approach has been to attribute the differences in implied volatilities to the differences in risk preferences.

Jackwerth presents both approaches and in a style that is rigorous but, despite the technical nature of the material, readily accessible to practitioners. Moreover, Jackwerth, unlike the quintessential ivory tower academic who views the real world as an uninteresting, special case of his model, takes care to offer many practical insights into how practitioners can use this information to improve their understanding of markets.

Although this material is not light reading, Jackwerth is particularly considerate of the nonexpert in two ways. He offers a glossary of technical terms, and he collects the seriously technical material in two appendixes. Whether you specialize in options trading or simply want a better understanding of some of the fascinating world of options, you will be very well served by this excellent monograph. The Research Foundation is especially pleased to present *Option-Implied Risk-Neutral Distributions and Risk Aversion.*

Mark Kritzman, CFA
Research Director
The Research Foundation of the
Association for Investment Management and Research

Preface

Since about 1994, considerable interest has been shown in academia and the central banks in "option-implied risk-neutral distributions." The purpose of this Research Foundation monograph is to provide some insight into the use of such a concept for the investment professional. Much of the work in this field is mathematically complex, requires advanced tools of financial economics, and is written with fellow researchers rather than practitioners in mind. The goal of this monograph is to bridge the gap between academia and practice by explaining what can and what cannot be learned from option prices for applications in financial analysis. As part of this goal, I provide step-by-step examples so that the reader can actually apply these concepts.

Fundamentally, the concept of learning from option prices, which underlies the estimation of the risk-neutral distribution, is not new. Investment professionals have always appreciated prices for the information they contain. For example, a high price of IBM shares compared with their historical levels indicates that investors value IBM highly. We might not know why, but that information alone (that other investors think highly of IBM) is important news to us. Consider a different example: If we know the value of futures contracts written on an index and know the value of the index (because shares historically did not have futures written on them), we can also infer the risk-free interest rate as the ratio of the futures value and ex dividend index value. Similarly, we have long been accustomed to using bond prices to infer the term structure of spot and forward rates, from which we can speculate about future spot interest rates. In this case, we are learning from each bond price about a particular interest rate.

We can think of security prices as some kind of expected value of future cash flows (the exact nature of the expectation is at this point irrelevant for the argument, and I will address it later in great detail). Then, each price tells us a little bit about the probability distribution from which we take those expectations. One price (say, the futures price) will yield one piece of information about the probability distribution. In the simple case of only one futures price, the price information will yield the location of that distribution—that is, the expected value that is the risk-free rate in this example. That the expected return under our distribution is the risk-free rate, not the mean index return, might come as a surprise. The explanation is that for pricing purposes, we use a different distribution from the actual probability distribution; we use the risk-neutral distribution. I return to the exact nature of this risk-neutral distribution in the following pages.

When we are able to examine *option prices* in addition to the stock price, we gain with each option price one more piece of information about the risk-neutral probability distribution. For example, with four options written on a share, all of which expire at the same time but all of which have different strike prices, we have information about four moments of the distribution—quite a lot of information, which we can use to depict the risk-neutral distribution. So, although learning from prices about the location of the distributions of future security prices is an old concept, its application to options is new and rich. Options allow us to learn much more about the shape of the risk-neutral distribution.

A final application is to compare the option-inferred risk-neutral distributions with estimated actual distributions of stock prices based on, for example, the historical price path. The relationship between these two distributions depends on the preferences (utilities) of investors about money as they grow richer or poorer. Knowing both distributions allows us to infer what the preferences must be within an economy to be consistent with option prices and historical returns.

Where does all this research and information leave the investment professional? Although a great deal can be learned from option prices, we need to establish what can be reasonably well analyzed (the center of the option-implied risk-neutral probability distribution) and what cannot (individual preferences or actual movements of security prices). What this monograph tries to achieve is a clear demonstration for practitioners of what can be reasonably inferred from option prices, how to do that, and what pitfalls to avoid. Another issue is the interpretation of this information. If we are observing only the risk-neutral distribution, we must be careful not to immediately apply it for forecasting actual events. For such forecasts, the actual distribution must be used. So, the monograph will detail the rules governing when and how to use the option-implied risk-neutral distribution. Finally, the monograph unveils an empirical irregularity, the "pricing kernel puzzle," which suggests that the risk-neutral distribution, the actual distribution, and the implied preferences are incompatible with each other. An implication of this puzzle is that money can be made if some securities are mispriced. I spell out in detail what kinds of strategies may be profitable.

I usually identify terms as the discussion develops, but because a number of the terms in the monograph might not be familiar to the reader, I have collected them in a glossary that briefly explains each one. Terms that are included in the glossary are in small capital letters when they are first mentioned in the text or exhibits.

This monograph is organized in the following manner. First, I discuss why financial analysts might be interested in learning about the economy from option prices. I also provide a brief history of option pricing. Next, the monograph explores the empirical problems of the Black–Scholes (1973) model, especially after the 1987 market crash, and investigates potential explanations for the behavior of observed option prices. The monograph then introduces risk-neutral option pricing and the theoretical underpinnings of asset pricing in complete and incomplete markets. The concept of the risk-neutral probability distribution formally introduced at this point is central to the rest of the monograph. The stage is now set for a thorough discussion of the "inverse problem," which concerns how to obtain risk-neutral implied distributions from observed market option prices. Then, the discussion turns to the question of what stochastic processes are consistent with a particular terminal risk-neutral distribution. Binomial trees are particularly simple examples of such stochastic processes, but I also present extensions and alternative approaches. By building on the theory presented earlier, I can now use the ratio of the risk-neutral implied distribution and the actual distribution to estimate economywide scaled marginal utility functions (pricing kernels), a methodology that is described thoroughly before the concluding section.

For helpful discussions related to the monograph, I would like to thank Kostas Iordanidis and Mark Rubinstein. Generous funding by the AIMR Research Foundation is gratefully acknowledged. I am also thankful to Mark Kritzman, the Foundation's research director. This monograph is based in part on an earlier article (Jackwerth 1999), and I am grateful to Institutional Investor for permission to use the 1999 article in this way.

Option-Implied Risk-Neutral Distributions and Risk Aversion

In introducing the motivation behind this monograph, I would like to turn usual security valuation and OPTION-pricing theory upside down. For the longest time, practitioners and academics were content with pricing securities based on models that made specific assumptions about the evolution of security prices. Often, we assumed a GEOMETRIC BROWNIAN MOTION to describe security prices. The resulting model-based security prices were then used for trading.[1] But traders soon realized that some market prices did not adhere to the model prices. Rubinstein (1985) documented the first such widespread violations of model prices. We came to realize that our stylized models do not account for all facets of the real world. The fact that the real world is much richer in patterns and processes seems obvious, but only recently has this appreciation been translated into reversing the direction of reasoning: It is no longer from an assumed model toward theoretical prices but from observed market prices to the implied distributions and STOCHASTIC processes that could have generated them.

The reasons for this change in perspective are manifold. For one, our trust in market prices increased as exchanges became more common and more reliable. Data are more widely available nowadays. Especially for equity options, researchers detected pronounced deviations of observed prices from model prices starting after the crash of 1987. Finally, mathematical sophistication and computational power became available to tackle the so-called inverse problem: What information about the economy and security processes is contained in a set of market prices?

Before venturing to answer that question, I would like to spend some time on the history of option pricing up to the turning point—that is, the crash of 1987.[2] Options have been with us for a long time. One of the first examples comes from around 550 B.C. in ancient Greece, where CALL OPTIONS on olive presses gave the owner of the options, Thales of Miletus, the right to use all the olive-pressing capacity in Chios and Miletus after the harvest. Through most of history, options were traded—as in the 1870s in New York, for

[1] In the case of options, these models would begin with the famous Black–Scholes (1973) model for pricing options.

[2] More detailed accounts can be found in Benhamou (2003) and Margrabe (2002).

example—between buyers and sellers as over-the-counter instruments. Some exchanges, however, traded options as early as the 17th century (Amsterdam), and Bachelier (1900) reported option trading on the Paris exchange around 1900. The situation changed fundamentally on 26 April 1973, when the Chicago Board Options Exchange (CBOE) introduced exchange-traded options. Trading volume grew rapidly, and other exchanges were soon also offering option contracts.

Analysis of the pricing of options largely paralleled this development. In the beginning, investors had to think about how much an option would be worth to them without the benefit of a mathematical model; prices tended to be the result of educated guesses, because liquid markets did not exist. Prices of options were higher than would be produced from modern models and higher than present-day market prices, indicating the presence of a substantial RISK PREMIUM to compensate the writer of the option for the trouble of providing such a rare security that was so difficult to value.

Bachelier was the first to develop a theoretical model to price options. Having been a student of the mathematician Poincare, he assumed that a stock price evolves over time as an arithmetic BROWNIAN MOTION. The required assumptions were themselves problematic; they stipulated normally distributed stock prices that could become negative and ignored dividends and interest rates. Despite these drawbacks, his work was far ahead of its time because it was based on probabilistic assumptions about the evolution of stock prices. Nobody else thought in such a way about stock prices at the time, and his thesis was promptly forgotten until the middle of the 20th century.

At that time, Osborne (1959) advocated geometric Brownian motion as the model for asset prices. At this point, a mathematical model of option pricing could finally be derived. Under the assumption of geometric Brownian motion, we know that the stock price at some terminal date will be lognormally distributed. Also, we can calculate the payoff of the option for each realization of the underlying stock price. We can then calculate the expected payoff of the option by multiplying each payoff at a given stock price by the likelihood of that payoff occurring and subsequently summing across all stock prices.

An important ingredient was still missing at this point. Bachelier completely ignored appreciation of the stock, but simply using the expected rate of return on the stock is also not correct. The reason is that the utility of the investor—that is, the investor's attitude toward risk taking—plays a role in pricing when risky payoffs are involved, as is the case with an option. The way risk-averse investors treat an additional dollar depends on the investors' wealth at any time. When investors are poor, they will pay more for that additional dollar than when they are rich. These concepts were developed for financial applications starting in the late 1950s by, among others, Sharpe (1964) and Samuelson (1965). Incorporating utility theory's concept of risk aversion is an essential part of Sprenkle's (1964) option-pricing formula:

$$C = e^{\rho T}(S)N\left[\frac{\ln(S/K) + (\rho + \sigma^2/2)T}{\sigma\sqrt{T}}\right] - (1-Z)(K)N\left[\frac{\ln(S/K) + (\rho - \sigma^2/2)T}{\sigma\sqrt{T}}\right], \quad (1)$$

where

C = value of the call option
ρ = average rate of growth of the share price
T = time to maturity of the option
S = share price
$N(\cdot)$ = cumulative standard normal distribution function
K = exercise price of the option
σ = volatility of the stock returns
Z = degree of risk aversion

Slightly varying models were built by Boness (1964), Samuelson, and Thorp and Kassouf (1967).

The Sprenkle formula involved the expected return on the asset, r, and incorporated an adjustment for risk aversion, Z. The formula was thus unwieldy because analysts normally do not know the economywide coefficient of risk aversion. Also, early investors realized that the Sprenkle formula did not work well for pricing the existing options of the time. An *ad hoc* adjustment could be made, however, by setting risk aversion to zero, replacing the expected return on the stock with the risk-free rate, and discounting the resulting option price at the risk-free rate.

Not until the seminal work of Black and Scholes and of Merton (1973), however, could analysts have a clear theoretical understanding of why the risk-free rate should be used for discounting instead of the expected return on the asset. The short explanation is that in COMPLETE MARKETS, investors can hedge their exposure to an option by an offsetting position in the stock and the bond. But if any investor can costlessly eliminate the risk of the option position, then the expected return should be only the risk-free rate.

Black developed this idea when he applied the capital asset pricing model (CAPM) to option pricing. He was pointed in this direction by Jack Treynor, who suggested the use of a Taylor series expansion. The personal risk aversion of the investor no longer mattered in this approach because any risk could be hedged. In particular, Black and Scholes realized that the expected return on the stock did not appear in the option-pricing formula anymore and could thus be set to any value. The risk-free rate turned out to be a convenient choice because it represents how a risk-neutral investor would discount. Thus, the terms "risk-neutral pricing" and "risk-neutral distribution" were introduced. The resulting Black–Scholes formula is

$$C = (S)N\left[\frac{\ln(S/K) + (r + \sigma^2/2)T}{\sigma\sqrt{T}}\right] - e^{-rT}(K)N\left[\frac{\ln(S/K) + (r - \sigma^2/2)T}{\sigma\sqrt{T}}\right], \quad (2)$$

where r is the risk-free interest rate.

This formula was a breakthrough theoretically and in practical terms because all inputs to the Black–Scholes formula were observable except the VOLATILITY parameter, which could be estimated from historical stock returns.[3] Merton's particular contribution was to show mathematically how one can hedge all risks, not just the systematic risk of the CAPM with which Black and Scholes were concerned. The explosive growth of the options industry was fueled by the advent of large organized exchanges at the same time and the development of an efficient numerical scheme by Cox, Ross, and Rubinstein (1979). We will look at that scheme in more detail in the section "Implied Binomial Trees."

In the wake of development of the Black–Scholes formula, many extensions were proposed. Almost immediately, Merton introduced models that incorporated stochastic interest rates, dividends, changes in STRIKE PRICES, American-style exercise before expiration, and a down-and-out call. Other extensions involved applications to corporate debt, futures, currencies, options to exchange one asset for another, options on the minimum and maximum of several assets, and a variety of other specialized options. Two more modern developments came with the introduction of stochastic volatility by Heston (1993) and the addition of stochastic jumps and stochastic interest rates by Bates (1996, 2000, 2001).

The basic modeling direction, however, was not fundamentally changed. Researchers always started out with a stochastic process that described the evolution of the underlying asset. Then, they worked out the risk-neutral dynamics of that stochastic process (e.g., changing the discount rate from the expected return on the asset in the Sprenkle formula to the risk-free rate in the Black–Scholes case). The final option-pricing model was then the discounted expected value of the option payoff under the RISK-NEUTRAL PROBABILITY distribution.

This way of thinking changed with the advent of exchange-traded options in the early 1970s. As option prices became available in large quantities,

[3]Merton and Scholes received the Nobel Prize for the pricing model in 1997; Black's death in 1995 prevented him from joining his colleagues.

investors began to reverse the process of obtaining prices from models to working out the implied model parameters that were consistent with observed prices. They calculated implied Black–Scholes volatilities, which are needed as inputs to the Black–Scholes formula to arrive at the observed market prices. The IMPLIED VOLATILITY of an option is simply that volatility that makes the model price exactly equal to the observed market price. Each option has a unique implied volatility, and traders like to quote options in terms of implied volatilities. The main reason is that as the underlying asset price changes through the day, the implied volatility does not have to be adjusted as much as the option prices, which change all the time.

The only way to calculate implied volatilities is through an iterative procedure based on a Newton–Raphson search.[4] Manaster and Koehler (1982) worked out the details and a starting value that guarantees convergence. Hentschel (2003) noted that implied volatilities suffer from biases if option prices are observed with such errors as finite quote precision, BID–ASK SPREADS, or nonsynchronous prices. A further upward bias results from a censoring of low prices that violate no-arbitrage bounds. These problems are most prevalent for away-from-the-money options, and Hentschel derived optimal weighting schemes to mitigate these errors in implied volatilities.

The novel aspect in calculating implied volatilities is that equilibrium market prices are now being used to learn about the stochastic process of the underlying asset and its probability distribution rather than this process being assumed. This monograph investigates these recent developments and describes what we can learn from observed option prices about the economy we live in.

Empirical Findings

We start with a description of the empirical regularities of the implied volatilities in different markets. Many of the results hint at the fact that the Black–Scholes model might not hold perfectly in the real world. Thus, we investigate potential explanations for deviations from the Black–Scholes model.

Empirical Problems with Black–Scholes. Ever since investors have been calculating implied volatilities, they have also plotted them across strike prices for options with the same time to expiration and on the same underlying stock. These plots are called (implied) volatility "smiles." According to the Black–Scholes formula, the VOLATILITY SMILE should be a flat line because only one volatility parameter governs the underlying stochastic process on which all options are priced. Rubinstein (1985) did indeed find that the volatility

[4]A Newton–Raphson search is an iterative procedure for finding the roots of a function.

smiles for options on individual U.S. stocks are more or less flat. Although he found slightly U-shaped volatility smiles for individual stock options, the violations of the Black–Scholes model were mainly within the bid–ask spreads. An investor would thus not be able to trade profitably on these deviations.

The same holds for European-style options on the U.S. S&P 500 Index, which were flat from the start of their exchange-based trading in April 1986 until the U.S. stock market crash of October 1987. After the crash, however, volatility smiles became skewed; that is, volatility smiles became downward sloping as the strike price increased. A set of typical volatility smiles for four international indexes is given in **Figure 1**. The graph is presented (as normally) in terms of "moneyness"—that is, the ratio of strike price to index level. Note that the volatility smile tends to flatten out and can even increase again on the right-hand side. As Figure 1 shows, this pattern is not unique to the U.S. index option market. Tompkins (2001) supported these findings and also found downward-sloping smiles for the Japanese market, even where the smile is flat for the particular day considered in Figure 1.

Other markets also often exhibit volatility smiles. Toft and Prucyk (1997) and Mayhew (1995) found downward-sloping volatility smiles for individual stock options, although the curves were not nearly as steep as in the index smiles. Campa, Chang, and Reider (1998) and Bollen and Rasiel (2002) found that foreign exchange options often exhibit U-shaped volatility smiles, albeit covering a range of implied volatilities of only 2–3 percent (as opposed to 20 percent for the index options). The same U-shape is also often found in interest rate markets, and Jarrow, Li, and Zhao (2003) reported a downward-sloping volatility smile for the interest rate caps market.

Potential Explanations. Many solutions have been offered to explain the downward sloping and, to a lesser extent, the U-shaped volatility smiles. Black (1976), Christie (1982), and Schwert (1989) first described the leverage effect. When the price of its stock falls, the corporation's debt-to-equity ratio increases because debt stays constant while equity is being reduced. If a shock of the same size happens to asset prices before and after the fall in asset prices, the impact of the shock on equity is larger after the fall in asset values. Thus, volatility is higher for low strike prices. Toft and Prucyk argued, however, that the leverage effect is a rather minor effect that can explain only about half of the already relatively flat smiles of individual U.S. stock options. Thus, it would explain even less of the steep index option smiles.

Grossman (1988), Gennotte and Leland (1990), Guidolin and Timmermann (2000), and Romer (1993) suggested solving the enigma of the volatility smile by using models with information aggregation. In these models investors learn about the true value of the underlying asset through trading, and

Figure 1. Empirical Volatility Smiles on Four International Indexes

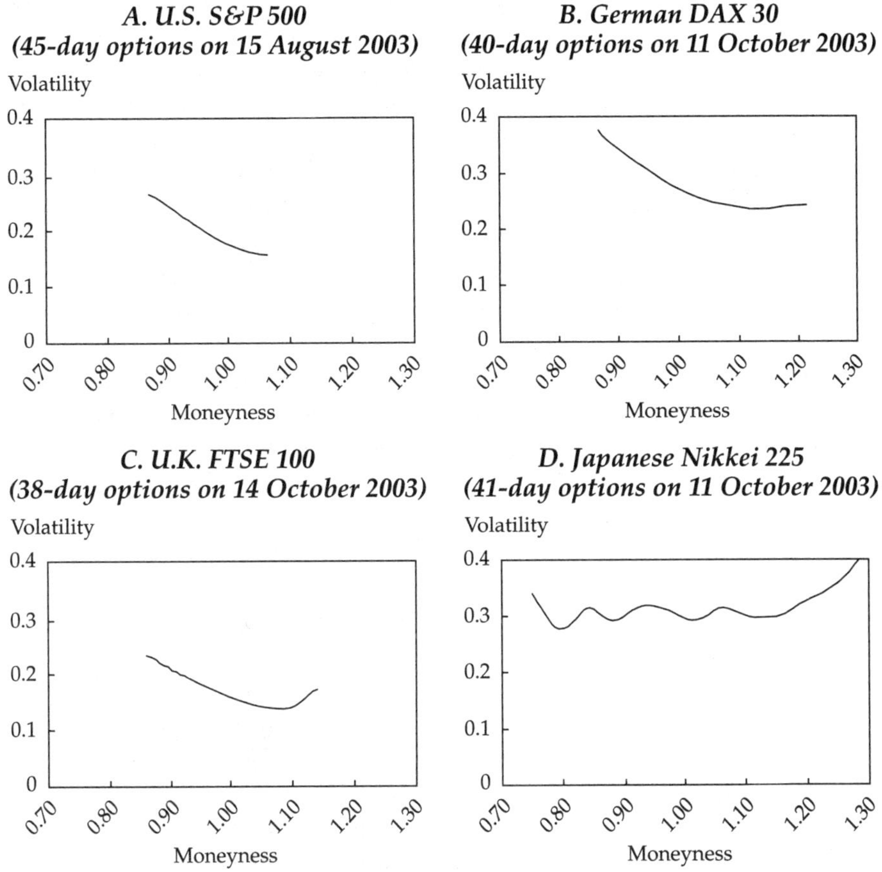

Note: Moneyness = Strike price/Index level.

prices adjust rapidly once learning takes place. Unfortunately, according to these models, decreases in asset prices are as likely as increases in asset prices, whereas the downward-sloping volatility smile suggests that decreases in asset prices are more likely than increases. The smile is thus more in tune with our understanding that markets sometimes melt down but rarely ever "melt up." On a downward-sloping volatility smile, the OUT-OF-THE-MONEY PUTS are relatively expensive. Those PUT OPTIONS essentially provide portfolio insurance; that is, they pay off when the market crashes. The options are thus priced in such a way that they incorporate some investors' fear that market crashes are rather likely.

Kelly (1994) suggested that the correlations between stocks increase in down markets, thereby reducing the diversification effect of a portfolio. Thus, indexes experience higher volatility in down markets.[5]

Another explanation for the volatility smile could be that investors are more risk averse in down markets than what is commonly believed by economists. Franke, Stapleton, and Subrahmanyam (1999) achieved such an effect through the introduction of undiversifiable background risk, whereas Benninga and Mayshar (1997) achieved it through studying a setup with heterogeneous investors. Similarly, Grossman and Zhou (1996) modeled heterogeneous investors with one group exogenously demanding portfolio insurance. Also working with heterogeneous investors and in a setting where some are crash averse and demand portfolio insurance (à la Grossman and Zhou), Bates (2001) showed that a jump DIFFUSION PROCESS can generate a volatility smile. All these models generate only rather moderately sloped volatility smiles, however, and do not explain the steep volatility skews in the indexes.

Pindyck (1984), French, Schwert, and Stambaugh (1987), and Campbell and Hentschel (1992) developed models with volatility feedback. In these models, negative news leads to a decrease in asset prices and to an increase in volatility, which, in turn, leads to an increase in the EQUITY RISK PREMIUM. The increased risk premium further depresses asset prices, which again feeds the increase in volatility.

A promising group of models suggests that the price of the underlying asset follows a stochastic diffusion process, with additional factors such as stochastic volatility, stochastic interest rates, or stochastic jumps. Such models were offered by Bates (2000), Bakshi, Cao, and Chen (1997), and Pan (2002).

So far, the literature has revealed no consensus as to which of these explanations matters the most empirically. One of the rare studies of this issue is the research of Dennis and Mayhew (2000), but their results are not strong: A number of explanatory variables seem to matter, but no "smoking gun" is in sight. Moreover, although some of these models can indeed generate downward-sloping volatility smiles, they normally introduce the same pattern into the probability distribution of the actual stochastic process. In this case, both the risk-neutral distribution implied from option prices, which is determined by the implied volatility smile and vice versa, and the actual distribution of asset returns will be left skewed and leptokurtic. That is, they will have a large left tail (a higher likelihood of crashes) and they will be more peaked than a (log)normal distribution. We revisit this connection theoretically and

[5]As a statistical aside, Campbell, Koedijk, and Kofman (2002) showed that sensible conditioning here should be with respect to the portfolio return being smaller than a threshold, not with respect to individual asset returns.

empirically in the section "Implied Risk Aversion." Here, note that the actual distribution looks empirically rather lognormal, does not exhibit a large left tail, and is not leptokurtic.

Where does that leave us? We are in the uncomfortable situation that the simple assumptions of the Black–Scholes model seem to be violated in a number of subtle ways. Market microstructure–related effects provide little explanation, but the leverage effect (at least for companies) seems to have some explanatory power. Other reasons—such as the beta of a stock—have some small impact. Some explanations—such as the negative volatility feedback—are too simplistic because they do not provide for a clear way for the stock to recover from the high-volatility regime. Also, the implied volatility smiles in many markets are not pronounced. Additionally, there is the question of whether the violations are even beyond the bid–ask spreads in many cases. In the case of U-shaped volatility smiles, we also need to consider that those options that are far away from the money have little value and any small transaction cost would increase their prices considerably.

We do have one particular market, however, that exhibits a striking volatility smile. The downward-sloping index volatility smile is much steeper than in any other market, and deviations are much larger than the bid–ask spread. Here, the existing models have little explanatory power and the market prices might exhibit systematic deviations that can be profitably exploited. We examine this issue in the section "Implied Risk Aversion."

Risk-Neutral Pricing

From this section, we first need to understand the economic underpinnings of risk-neutral pricing. Once we have a simple model in place, we can turn to the inverse problem of recovering risk-neutral probabilities from option prices in complete markets. Finally, we will consider the inverse problem in incomplete markets. We can then appreciate the connection between actual probabilities, risk-neutral probabilities, and preferences—which will be crucial for the remainder of this monograph.

Consider a simple economy in which the stock can evolve into one of only two states in the future—in this case, in one year (i.e., the stock price evolution is modeled as a one-step BINOMIAL TREE). The current stock price is 1. In the up state, the stock price is 1.2214, and in the down state, it is 0.8187. The actual probabilities of the two states are 0.9 and 0.1, respectively. The bond is priced at 1 today and has a price of 1.1 in either of the two future states. This economy is depicted in **Figure 2**.

If we now want to value an AT-THE-MONEY CALL on the stock—that is, a call with a strike price of 1—we can naively calculate the discounted expected

Figure 2. Simple One-Period, Two-State Economy

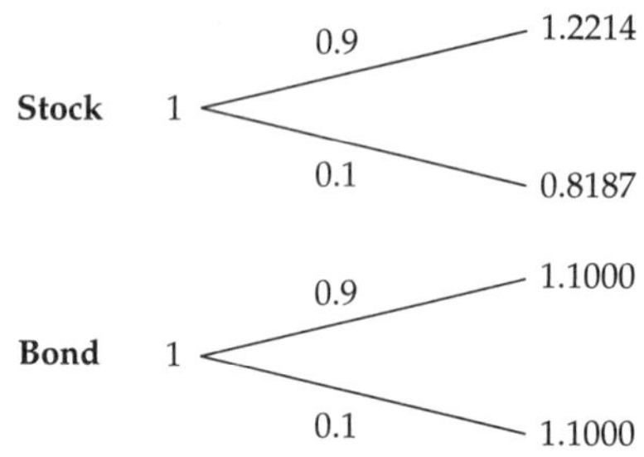

payoff (= max of 0 and the stock price minus the strike price) under the actual probabilities. The payoff in the up state is 0.2214, and in the down state, it is 0. The expected payoff is, therefore, $0.9 \times 0.2214 + (0.1 \times 0) = 0.1993$. The bond prices imply a risk-free rate of 10 percent, so the discounted expected payoff of the call is $0.1993/1.1 = 0.1811$. The true price of the call, however, is only 0.1406.

The reason for the difference is that investors receive the payoff from the call in the up state when they are already wealthy. In that state, they have less appreciation for additional cash flows and will accordingly pay less for the call. Therefore, to work out the true price of the call, we must turn to the concept of STATE PRICES. The up-state price is what an investor is willing to pay for the certain payment of 1.00 in the up state, and similarly, the down state has a state price. With the two existing securities, the stock and the bond, and two state prices, π_u and π_d, we have a so-called complete market (one with the same number of states as securities and with linearly independent payoffs) and can set up a system of equations as follows: For the stock,

$$1 = \pi_u 1.2214 + \pi_d 0.8187, \tag{3a}$$

and for the bond,

$$1 = \pi_u 1.1000 + \pi_d 1.1000. \tag{3b}$$

Equation 3a says that the stock is worth its payoff in the up state, valued with the state price that we are paying for receiving 1.00 in that state, plus its payoff in the down state, valued at the state price that we are paying for receiving 1.00 in that state. The second equation values the bond. The solutions to this system of equations are $\pi_u = 0.6350$ and $\pi_d = 0.2741$.

The sum of the state prices has to be equal to the price of a bond, which pays 1.00 in each state (1/1.1 = 0.9091). Then, a convenient step is to multiply the state prices by the inverse of the price of this unit bond. The resulting risk-neutral probabilities, P_i, then sum to 1:

$$P_i = r^T \pi_i, \tag{4}$$

where r is 1 plus the annual interest rate of the unit bond (risk-free rate) and T is the terminal date when the payoffs occur. The risk-neutral probabilities in this example are

$$P_u = 0.6350 \times 1.1 = 0.6985$$

and

$$P_d = 0.2741 \times 1.1 = 0.3015.$$

We can now calculate the value, C, of any security with payoff X_i at time T by calculating the discounted expectation under the risk-neutral probabilities (or simply using the state prices right away):

$$\begin{aligned} C &= \frac{\sum_i P_i X_i}{r^T} \\ &= \sum_i \pi_i X_i . \end{aligned} \tag{5}$$

The true value of the call is found to be indeed

$$\frac{(0.6985 \times 0.2214) + (0.3015 \times 0)}{1.1} = 0.1406.$$

Two observations are important at this point. First, any security with payoff at T in our economy can be priced once we know the risk-neutral distribution. Second, the ratio of state prices to actual probabilities is also called the PRICING KERNEL or STOCHASTIC DISCOUNT FACTOR. The pricing kernel, m, tells us about the marginal utility of the representative investor in a particular future state of the economy: The poorer the investor, the higher the ratio; the wealthier the investor, the lower the ratio.

Using the definition of $m = \pi / Q$, where Q is the actual probability, we can rewrite the pricing equation. With the help of the pricing kernel, we can value securities as expected scaled payoffs under the actual probabilities. In this valuation, the pricing kernel provides for the scaling:

$$\begin{aligned} C &= \left(\frac{\sum_i P_i X_i}{r^T}\right) \\ &= \sum_i \frac{Q_i}{Q_i}\pi_i X_i \\ &= \sum_i Q_i m_i X_i . \end{aligned} \tag{6}$$

In the example, the pricing kernel is

$$\frac{0.2741}{0.1} = 2.7410 \text{ in the down state}$$

and

$$\frac{0.6350}{0.9} = 0.7056 \text{ in the up state.}$$

Thus, when the investor is poor, he or she treats 1.00 received as if it happened with about three times the likelihood that it really did happen. When the investor is rich, he or she treats 1.00 received as if it happened with only about three-quarters of the likelihood that it really did. Such an investor is risk averse because he or she does not like exposure to the down state at all and is willing to pay to avoid it. For a risk-averse investor, the pricing kernel is decreasing in wealth, as is the case here (2.7 in the down state and 0.71 in the up state).

Consider now the recovery of risk-neutral probabilities from option prices, after which we will return to the concept of marginal utility and the associated pricing kernel puzzle.

Complete Markets. Complete markets are markets with exactly as many securities (with linearly independent payoffs) as possible future states. The preceding example had such a market with two states and two securities. If the security prices in a complete market do not exhibit arbitrage opportunities (that is, an investor cannot make money for sure and there is no riskless "free lunch"), then one can always recover a unique set of risk-neutral probabilities. Ross (1976) was one of the first researchers to investigate such complete markets when he focused on the special case of a market with a complete set of EUROPEAN OPTIONS, one for each state. Closely related is the result presented by Breeden and Litzenberger (1978) that concerned the case of a continuum of call options, so that the option prices can be expressed as a function $C(K)$ across strike prices K. Breeden and Litzenberger went on to derive an exact formula for the state prices as a function of future stock prices. The state price for the state in which stock price S is equal to a strike price K

then obtains as the second derivative of the call price function (if we use forward call prices, we obtain the risk-neutral probability distribution right away):

$$\frac{\partial^2 C}{\partial K^2} = \pi_{S=K} \Leftrightarrow \frac{\partial^2 r^T C}{\partial K^2} = P_{S=K}. \tag{7}$$

Of course, possible states of the world tend to be much more numerous than existing securities, so complete markets rarely exist. If investors can rebalance their portfolios over time, however, as the states are being revealed, then they can use the concept of *dynamically* complete markets. For example, imagine a state space with four states and two securities, a stock and a bond. The market is incomplete, so rather than one set of risk-neutral probabilities, we have infinitely many of them. But now assume we can trade at an intermediate point in time and that the stock price can, over any short time span, move only up or down. **Figure 3** shows this pattern.

Figure 3. Two-Period Binomial Tree

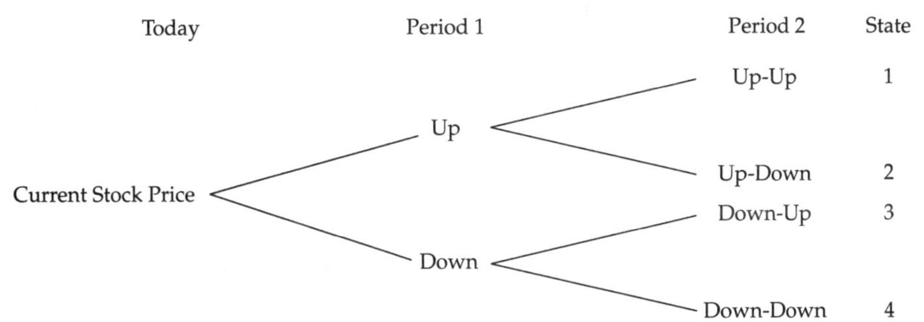

In the first period, we can move only up or down. In the second period, if we first moved up, we now have paths up-up and up-down. If we first moved down, we have the paths down-up and down-down. So, as we had in the situation without intermediate trading, we again have four possible terminal states. With the bond in the mixture, however, we have three locally complete markets, each with two securities and two states over each short-time interval.

As long as we can costlessly rebalance our stock and bond portfolio at each instant of time, we need only two securities to dynamically complete this market. That is, for each sequence of up/down moves that describes one path of the stock price, a dynamic hedging strategy exists and a state price is associated with that path. This setup is the basis for the Cox, Ross, and Rubinstein standard binomial tree model and its extensions.

Still, most markets are not even dynamically complete. Thus, we face the problem of recovering the risk-neutral distribution in incomplete markets.

Incomplete Markets. Incomplete markets exist for many reasons. Position limits and short-sale restrictions can lead to incomplete markets, as can trading costs. The asset price may be driven by additional stochastic factors—such as stochastic volatility, stochastic interest rates, or stochastic jumps—that are not traded. In all of these cases, an investor cannot exactly replicate the payoff of an option state by state. In terms of risk-neutral probability distributions, the result is multiple risk-neutral distributions, all of which can price all existing assets correctly. Pricing a new security—one that is currently not being traded (a call option)—with these multiple risk-neutral distributions will yield a range of option prices between a lower and an upper bound.

To illustrate, I will extend the two-state, two-security setting and introduce a new intermediate state in which the stock price remains at 1. We are now faced with an incomplete market with two securities but three states. To obtain the lower and upper bounds (subject to pricing the stock and the bond correctly and subject to keeping all state prices nonnegative to avoid arbitrage violations), we minimize (and maximize) option price C of an at-the-money call option by varying the state prices:

$$\begin{aligned}
&\min\ (\max)\ C \\
&1 = \pi_u 1.2214 + \pi_m 1.0000 + \pi_d 0.8187 \\
&1 = \pi_u 1.1000 + \pi_m 1.1000 + \pi_d 1.1000 \\
&C = \pi_u 0.2214 + \pi_m 0.0000 + \pi_d 0.0000 \\
&\text{for } \pi_u, \pi_m, \text{ and } \pi_d \geq 0.
\end{aligned} \tag{8}$$

The lower bound on the call option price is 0.0909, with associated risk-neutral probabilities (that is, state prices times the risk-free rate) of 0.4517, 0.5483, and 0. The upper bound on the call option price is 0.1406, with associated risk-neutral probabilities of 0.6985, 0, and 0.3015. Any option price between the bounds can be obtained by varying the probabilities.

So far, we have imposed only the no-arbitrage condition that the state prices need to be positive. The resulting bounds are not tight but are already useful. To appreciate why we can back out risk-neutral probability distributions in incomplete markets and still obtain meaningful results, we now look at another example in which we impose only the no-arbitrage restriction. In this example, there are two options in the market, one at-the-money call option and one deep OUT-OF-THE-MONEY CALL option (this option has a strike price of 2), with prices of 0.25 and 0, respectively. The asset value is 1. We can view the underlying asset as a zero-strike option on itself and thus obtain the situation depicted in **Figure 4**.

The no-arbitrage bounds generated by the three option prices (the solid lines in Figure 4) yield two rather large triangular sections. A newly introduced

Figure 4. No-Arbitrage Bounds on Option Prices

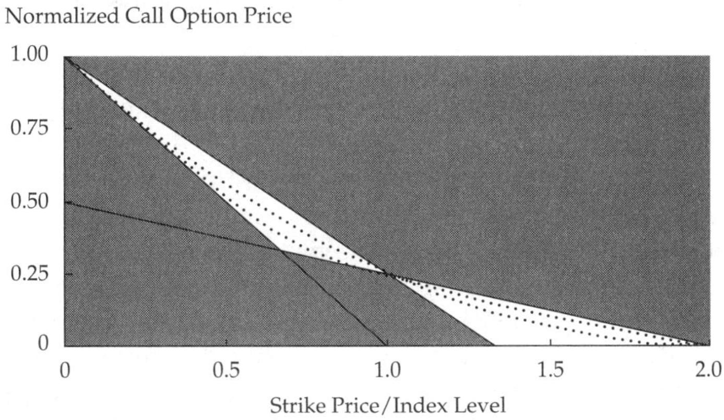

Note: All shaded areas represent arbitrage violation. Strike price/Index level = Moneyness.

option price would have to lie in either of those triangles to not violate the no-arbitrage condition. The resulting bounds on option prices based on only these three prices are so wide that they are virtually useless in real markets, but real market situations do often present 10 or more option prices close to at the money, which significantly tightens the bounds.

To improve these bounds, we call on the Breeden–Litzenberger result that the state price density is the second derivative of a convex call price function that must go through our three existing option prices. To obtain reasonable risk-neutral distributions, our call price functions themselves need to be fairly smooth. Two such candidate call price functions are plotted as the dotted lines in Figure 4. The possible locations for such smooth call price functions are much more limited than the no-arbitrage bounds. Thus, as long as we require that the risk-neutral distributions be not too erratic, we can obtain significantly tighter bounds on option prices.

The proposed additional restriction here (smoothness of the call price function or, equivalently, of the pricing kernel) is a novel suggestion. Other restrictions have been proposed in the literature. Perrakis (1986) and Ritchken (1985) were among the first to suggest that, in addition to keeping the state prices (or the pricing kernel) positive, one should also (to be consistent with risk-averse investors) require the pricing kernel to be monotonically decreasing in wealth. Violation of these bounds implies that risk-averse investors with increasing and concave utility of wealth can increase their utility by trading in the index, the risk-free rate, and the option in violation of the bounds.

Empirically, these bounds are not often violated because they are still not particularly tight; even the steep index volatility smile fits within the bounds most of the time.

Tightening these bounds by introducing more restrictions (and giving up the restriction on the monotonically decreasing pricing kernel), Bernardo and Ledoit (2000) and Cochrane and Saa-Requejo (2000) derived bounds on option prices through limits on the profitability of investments. Bernardo and Ledoit argued that restrictions should be put on the ratio of expected gains to expected losses, which limits how far the pricing kernel can deviate from a reference pricing kernel. The choice of this reference pricing kernel is a major problem because researchers do not agree on what the reference investor, whose pricing kernel is to be used, should be like. Cochrane and Saa-Requejo argued that the SHARPE RATIO (that is, expected excess return per unit of volatility) should be limited, a restriction that can be expressed in terms of a limit on the variability (variance) of the pricing kernel. This argument makes sense in equilibrium because extremely profitable opportunities should not exist in competitive markets (just as a free lunch as a result of arbitrage profits should not exist in equilibrium). Unfortunately, although Cochrane and Saa-Requejo could tighten the no-arbitrage bounds in some places, in others, they could achieve only the no-arbitrage bounds that we have already judged to be too loose.

Masson and Perrakis (2000) analyzed bounds on option prices when the underlying stochastic process includes a stochastic jump component. An important step toward increasing realism in a model is to derive bounds that allow intermediate trading (as opposed to buy-and-hold bounds). Constantinides and Perrakis (2002) provided such bounds, and empirical tests on S&P 500 options have shown that they are much tighter than existing bounds. Many more index options violated these bounds than violated the one-period bounds of Perrakis and of Ritchken. In another version of the Constantinides–Perrakis bounds, transaction costs caused the bounds to widen again when the investor had to pay transaction costs at each intermediate trading date. Nevertheless, we will find in the section "Implied Risk Aversion" some evidence that even static buy-and-hold strategies can earn abnormal profits in the index market when the volatility smile seems to be too steep.

The Inverse Problem

Knowledge of the risk-neutral probability distribution is desirable because it allows us to price any derivative of the particular underlying asset with the same time to expiration. Moreover, we can learn about the actual probabilities (for forecasting purposes) from the risk-neutral probability distribution through the link of the economywide scaled marginal utility (the pricing kernel). As a result, several methods have been developed to back out the risk-neutral probability distributions from option prices.

In this section, we investigate these approaches and their characteristics. The approaches selected are either particularly stable or easy to implement or both. Because all the existing models have some drawback, however, I propose a new and particularly simple algorithm that can be used for actual work. We then examine studies that have used risk-neutral distributions for forecasting and economic analysis. Finally, we turn to a practical question: How can investment professionals use these distributions to their advantage?

Because of the paucity of option prices in the 1970s and 1980s, not much empirical research was conducted at that time, so the history of recovering option-implied risk-neutral distributions is short. Banz and Miller (1978) highlight this problem. For purposes of capital budgeting, they backed risk-neutral probabilities out of a set of option prices, but in their example, they simply used hypothetical Black–Scholes-based option prices. As a result, they backed out the associated lognormal probabilities.

The next attempt to derive a histogram of risk-neutral probabilities from option prices was made by Longstaff (1990), who distributed the risk-neutral probability uniformly between any two adjacent strike prices. His method turned out to be numerically unstable, however, and yielded risk-neutral distributions for which the probabilities oscillated between large positive and large negative values. Mayhew investigated this problem and showed that the cause was the coarseness of the options data, which was observable only at discrete strikes. S&P 500 options have strike prices that differ by multiples of $5.00.

In the mid-1990s, research picked up as large options databases and powerful computers became available. In particular, the CBOE made the complete tick-by-tick options record from the early 1980s to 1995 available through the Berkeley Options Database. Unfortunately, the board stopped providing these valuable data at the end of 1995 and prohibited further sale of any of the data. Also, a number of research papers (e.g., Rubinstein 1994; Derman and Kani 1994) provided the theoretical background needed for the explosion in methods to recover the risk-neutral distribution.

From the multitude of these methods, we can discern two basic approaches: One is parametric, and the other is nonparametric. They have in common that the models of option prices developed in them depend on some number of variables that are moved around until they "best fit" the observed option prices.[6] Parametric approaches specify their models as functions of a

[6]As discussed later, "best" was defined in various ways—lowest absolute pricing error, lowest average error, and so on.

few (often, four) variables, whereas nonparametric models use many variables (usually 50 to 200 but up to 1,000 at times). The benefit of nonparametric models is the superior fit of option prices; the cost is unwieldy models that oscillate widely from one date to the next. The fluctuations are the result of overfitting, when small changes in market prices arising from noise in the data are fitted by the model.

Four articles are available to the reader who wants a deeper understanding of these methods—Cont (1997), Bahra (1997), Jackwerth (1999), and Perignon and Villa (2002). Cont focused on methods for obtaining the risk-neutral distributions, whereas the other surveys also covered applications. In this section, I follow a structure similar to that of Cont's and Jackwerth's; we will explore parametric methods first and nonparametric methods second.

Parametric Methods. In the simple parametric case, we pick a trial set of parameters for our risk-neutral probability distribution (e.g., a two-parameter lognormal distribution with known mean and volatility), price all options based on this distribution, and vary the parameters of the distribution to minimize the pricing error. This method has drawbacks if we use a parametric probability distribution that is not flexible enough for matching the observed option prices. As we have seen, the two-parameter lognormal distribution (on which the Black–Scholes model is based) is not sufficiently flexible to fit observed (index) option prices.

The specific models are categorized in **Exhibit 1**.[7] Within the parametric methods, we can identify three groups—expansion methods, generalized distribution methods, and mixture methods.

- *Expansion methods.* Expansion methods start with a simple known probability distribution (often normal or lognormal) and then add correction terms to it. Expansion methods are conceptually related to Taylor series expansions for simple functions. These correction terms are often not guaranteed to preserve the integrity of the probability distribution, so the user must always check that the resulting distribution is strictly positive and integrates to 1.
- *Generalized distribution methods.* Generalized distribution methods use distribution functions with more than the typical two parameters for the mean and the volatility; they often add SKEWNESS and KURTOSIS parameters. Skewness allows the (left) tail of the distribution to be fatter than the right tail

[7]Further detail is found in the references, but I strongly suggest using the nonparametric method described in the next section because it avoids the problems that afflict these parametric models.

Exhibit 1. Parametric Methods for Risk-Neutral Distributions

Author (year)	Category[a]	Base Distribution and Notes
Abadir and Rockinger (1997)	Exp –	CONFLUENT HYPERGEOMETRIC functions
Abken, Madan, and Ramamurtie (1996a, 1996b)	Exp +/–	Four-parameter HERMITE POLYNOMIALS
Aparicio and Hodges (1998)	Gen –	Beta function of the second kind
Brenner and Eom (1997)	Exp –	LAGUERRE POLYNOMIALS, corrections to gamma distribution
Corrado (2001)	Gen +/–	LAMBDA DISTRIBUTION
Corrado and Su (1996)	Exp +/–	GRAM–CHARLIER EXPANSION, normal distribution, two expansion terms
Corrado and Su (1997)	Exp +/–	Hermite polynomial with Gram–Charlier expansion
De Jong and Huisman (2000)	Gen +/–	Skewed Student *t*-distribution
Giamouridis and Tamvakis (2001, 2002)	Exp +/–	EDGEWORTH EXPANSION, lognormal distribution, two expansion terms
Jarrow and Rudd (1982)	Exp +/–	Edgeworth expansion, normal distribution, two expansion terms
Jondeau and Rockinger (2001)	Exp +/–	Hermite polynomial with Gram–Charlier expansion, restrictions added
Longstaff (1995)	Exp +/–	Edgeworth expansion, two expansion terms
Melick (1999)	Several	Survey of several methods applied to the same dataset
Melick and Thomas (1997)	Mix +	Three lognormal distributions
Posner and Milevsky (1998)	Gen +/–	JOHNSON FAMILY OF DENSITIES (see Johnson 1949 and Tadikamalla and Johnson 1982)
Potters, Cont, and Bouchaud (1998)	Exp +/–	Edgeworth expansion, single expansion term
Ritchey (1990)	Mix +	Mixture of normal distributions
Rubinstein (1998)	Exp +	Edgeworth expansion, binomial distribution, two expansion terms
Sherrick, Garcia, and Tirupattur (1995)	Gen +/–	BURR-TYPE DISTRIBUTION (see Burr 1942)
Sherrick, Irwin, and Forster (1992, 1996)	Gen +/–	Burr XII distribution
Young, Jabbour, Kramin, and Kramin (2001)	Exp +/–	Edgeworth expansion, normal distribution, two expansion terms

[a]Exp is for expansion, Gen is for generalized distribution, and Mix is for mixture; + indicates easy/reliable, +/– means normal, and – indicates difficult/unreliable.

to model the higher likelihood of melt-downs than melt-ups. Kurtosis allows the distribution to be more peaked in the center and to have fatter far tails at the expense of reduced probabilities in the near tails. Generalized distributions describe whole families of flexible distributions, which simplify to standard distributions for special parameter constellations.

■ *Mixture methods.* In mixture methods, one constructs probability distributions as weighted averages by adding several simple probability distributions with different mixing probabilities. The added flexibility comes at the cost of quickly increasing the number of parameters. A mixture of three lognormal distributions already yields eight parameters, two each for the three lognormal distributions and the two mixing probabilities. The third mixing probability results from the constraint that the three mixing probabilities must add up to 1. Moreover, mixture methods are prone to overfitting the data if the number of mixing distributions exceeds two or three. If overfitting has occurred, the resulting risk-neutral densities will exhibit sharp spikes (see, for example, Giamouridis and Tamvakis 2002).

Nonparametric Methods. In the nonparametric case, instead of picking a few parameters of a parametric risk-neutral probability distribution, we outright fit the risk-neutral probability distribution either pointwise or build it up from linear segments (or even from nonlinear pieces). The number of variables is much larger than in the parametric case. The particular exercise of fitting the risk-neutral distribution is rarely undertaken because it is difficult to constrain the probability distribution to be positive, to sum to 1, and to exhibit some smoothness. But in the few cases in which the probability distribution is being fitted directly, maximum ENTROPY methods (which are explained later) are most often used.

An improvement over the method of fitting the risk-neutral distribution straightaway is to fit a function of call option prices across strike prices and then use the Breeden–Litzenberger result to take two derivatives of the call price function with respect to strike prices and obtain the risk-neutral probability distribution after appropriate scaling. The drawback to this method is that call option prices vary greatly across strike prices: Deep IN-THE-MONEY CALLS are valued as high as the underlying asset itself, whereas deep out-of-the-money calls are valued close to zero. Thus, we are implicitly putting more weight on the in-the-money calls than on the out-of-the-money calls. Furthermore, we must ensure that the fitted function does not violate the arbitrage bounds, a requirement that often leads to numerical difficulties. Within this class of methods, KERNEL METHODS (explained later) are most often used.

A third and even better method is to fit the function of implied volatilities across strike prices. Then, calculating the function of call option prices from the implied *volatilities* is straightforward and one can proceed along the lines of Breeden and Litzenberger. The advantage of this method is that the implied volatilities are much more similar in magnitude across strike prices than call option prices are.[8] As long as the fitted volatility smiles do not change rapidly, these methods yield arbitrage-free risk-neutral probability distributions. Most of the better methods belong to this group, and typically, they use a procedure called "curve fitting," which is described later. The method of choice, the method I advocate, belongs to this group.

Specific nonparametric models are categorized in **Exhibit 2**, and the reader may want to investigate the references for details. Before turning to the method I suggest, we will look at the three groups of nonparametric methods—maximum entropy, kernel, and curve-fitting methods.

■ *Maximum entropy methods.* Maximum entropy methods find risk-neutral probability distributions that fit the options data and that presume the least information relative to a prior probability distribution. They try to maximize the amount of missing information, which is achieved by maximizing the cross-entropy:

$$-\sum_i P_i \ln\left(\frac{P_i}{O_i}\right), \tag{9}$$

where O_i is the prior probability distribution and P_i is the posterior risk-neutral probability distribution. As a prior distribution, a lognormal distribution is often chosen, and the resulting posterior distribution is subject to the constraints that the risk-neutral probabilities be strictly positive, that they sum to 1, and that they fit the option prices (with the underlying asset treated as a zero-strike option). If the prior distribution is uniform, the cross-entropy reduces to the simple entropy:

$$-\sum_i P_i \ln P_i. \tag{10}$$

The main problem with entropy methods lies in the use of the logarithm. Probabilities (and ratios of probabilities) can become tiny, and the logarithm of such small values goes rapidly to large negative values. Thus, the maximization will be dominated by those large negative values, which drive the result. Also, the method requires the use of nonlinear optimization routines, which tend to be finicky to operate and are not widely available to all practitioners.

■ *Kernel methods.* Kernel methods, used to fit the call price function and, at times, the implied volatility function, are related to nonlinear regressions.

[8]Keep in mind that in the Black–Scholes case, implied volatilities are all the same.

Exhibit 2. Nonparametric Methods for Risk-Neutral Distributions

Author (year)	Category[a]	Description and Notes
Aït-Sahalia and Lo (1998)	Ker +	Kernel estimator in stock price, strike, maturity, interest rate, and dividends
Andersen and Wagener (2002)	Cur +/–	Higher-order splines fitted to implied volatilities
Aparicio and Hodges (1998)	Cur +/–	Cubic B-splines fitted to implied volatilities
Bondarenko (2000)	Ker +/–	Convolution of kernel and standard densities
Branger (2002)	Max +/–	Maximum entropy
Brown and Toft (1999)	Cur +/–	Seventh-order splines fitted to implied volatilities
Buchen and Kelly (1996)	Max +/–	Maximum entropy with uniform and lognormal priors
Campa, Chang, and Reider (1998)	Cur +/–	Cubic splines fitted to implied volatilities
Härdle and Yatchew (2002)	Ker –	Nonparametric least squares through option prices
Hartvig, Jensen, and Pedersen (1999)	Cur +/–	Piecewise linear fit of log of the risk-neutral probability distribution
Hayes and Shin (2002)	Cur +/–	Cubic splines fitted to implied volatilities across deltas
Jackwerth (2000)	Cur +	Maximizing the smoothness of pointwise implied volatilities
Malz (1997)	Cur +	Quadratic polynomials fitted to implied volatilities across deltas
Mayhew (1995)	Cur +/–	Cubic splines fitted to implied volatilities
Pritsker (1998)	Ker +	Kernel estimator
Rockinger and Jondeau (2002)	Max +/–	Maximum entropy with normal, *t*, and generalized error distribution priors, added restrictions
Rookley (1997)	Ker +	Bivariate kernel in moneyness and time to expiration
Rosenberg (1998, 2003)	Cur +	Bivariate polynomial fitted to log implied volatilities
Rosenberg and Engle (2002)	Cur +	Polynomial fitted to log implied volatilities
Rubinstein (1994)	Max +/–	Maximum entropy with lognormal prior
Rubinstein (1994)	Cur +	Minimum distance between discrete and lognormal distribution
Shimko (1993)	Cur +	Quadratic polynomial fitted to implied volatilities
Stutzer (1996)	Max +/–	Maximum entropy with historical distribution as prior

[a]Ker is for kernel, Max is for maximum entropy, and Cur is for curve fitting; + indicates easy/reliable, +/– means normal, and – indicates difficult/unreliable.

They do not specify the linear form of a standard regression. Instead, they are localized. They start from the concept that each data point suggests the center of a region through which the function passes. The function is assumed to pass most likely right through the data point, and a kernel, $k(x)$, measures the likelihood that the function passes by the data point at a distance. A typical kernel is the standard normal distribution $n(x) = \left(1/\sqrt{2\pi}\right)e^{-0.5x^2}$, which measures the drop in likelihood of being further away from a data point.

Given an implied volatility smile with observations $\sigma_i(K_i)$, the volatility at strike price K is a weighted average of the implied volatilities in the vicinity of K—the farther away an observation, the less weight it is allotted, and vice versa. The formula for the kernel regression is

$$\sigma(K) = \frac{\sum_{i=1}^{n} k[(K-K_i)/h]\sigma_i}{\sum_{i=1}^{n} k[(K-K_i)/h]}, \qquad (11)$$

where h is the bandwidth. The bandwidth controls the trade-off between smoothness of the kernel regression and fitting the data. A reasonable starting point is $h = 0.9sn^{-1/5}$, where s is the standard deviation of the observations and n is the number of observations.[9] Kernel regressions tend to be data intensive and do not work well for bunched data that exhibit gaps. The problem is that the regression is not capable of fitting a smooth continuation of the function across the gap. Unfortunately, implied volatility smiles exhibit such gaps because observations are spaced according to the discrete strike prices. Pritsker used a kernel method for options on interest rates and documented a severe finite sample bias because of the persistence of interest rates. The asymptotic error bounds of Aït-Sahalia and Lo (1998) are, then, too tight.

■ *Curve-fitting methods.* Used primarily to fit the implied volatility function, curve-fitting methods try to fit the implied volatility smile with some flexible function. The most typical criteria for the fit are sums of the squared differences in modeled and observed volatilities, the squared differences in modeled and observed option prices, or the squares of 1 minus the ratio of option prices. Using the sum of squared differences in option prices puts more weight on in-the-money options; therefore, I suggest using the sum of squared differences in implied volatilities or the sum of squares of 1 minus the ratio of option prices. Also, Christoffersen and Jacobs (2001) argued that the error assessment should be consistent throughout fitting the risk-neutral probability distribution and that the same error assessment should then be used in pricing and forecasting applications. Because the shape of the risk-neutral distribution is not sensitive to the choice of difference measure, however, an analyst can use either one. Empirically, collecting as many option prices as possible is much more important than the difference measure.

---

[9]See Silverman (1986, p. 48), and for more detailed information, see Härdle (1990).

Typical functions for curve fitting are polynomials in the strike price [$\sigma(K) = \alpha_0 + \alpha_1 K + \alpha_2 K^2 + \ldots + \alpha_n K^n$], but they can exhibit oscillatory behavior if they involve higher-order terms. Here, SPLINES are a better choice; splines piece together polynomial segments at so-called knots by matching levels and derivatives at the knots. The choice of the location of those knots is somewhat of an art; too many knots cause overfitting of the data and too few knots prevent the observed volatilities from being matched. Splines tend to be smoother and do not exhibit the oscillations that polynomials are prone to, but they need to be of an order higher than 3 for the probability distribution to turn out to be smooth.

Shimko first proposed fitting a quadratic polynomial to the implied volatilities. He translated those implied volatilities into call option prices and then obtained the risk-neutral distribution through the Breeden–Litzenberger method. Because the tails contained no options data, he added lognormal tails to the risk-neutral distribution. Malz (1997) devised a variation of this method by fitting quadratic polynomials to implied volatilities across call OPTION DELTAS (that is, derivatives of call option prices with respect to the stock price) instead of strike prices. Numerically, the advantage of this method is that the range of feasible deltas is bounded by 0 and 1, whereas the strike price range is 0 to ∞. Translating from delta space, however, back to strike prices is cumbersome. In addition, taking the required two derivatives of the call options prices is much easier and more stable if one uses strike prices rather than deltas.

Alternatively, an analyst can explicitly fit smooth functions by penalizing jaggedness. One way is to add into the objective function a term based on the sum or integral of squared second derivatives of the function. The more curvature the function has, the larger this term will be. A trade-off parameter governs how much weight is given to fit versus smoothness. Its value is typically based on trial and error.

Nonparametric Methods Compared. The easiest and most stable methods tend to be in the group of methods for curve-fitting the implied volatility smile. The limiting case of a flat implied volatility function simply gives the Black–Scholes model. These methods tend to be exceedingly fast and some of them require only a single calculation. As long as the implied volatility smile is reasonably smooth, the associated risk-neutral probability distribution will be strictly positive. Because this condition is not guaranteed, however, it should be checked separately. Clark (2002) derived conditions under which the risk-neutral distribution will be arbitrage free, but they are even more complicated than simple checks for positivity. The new method that I will propose for fast and easy computation belongs to this group.

In the meantime, I argue that, given a reasonable number of observed options, the choice of method does not matter much, so the analyst might as well pick a particularly easy method. As mentioned, the risk-neutral probability distributions are limited by the no-arbitrage bounds on option prices. The bounds on an individual option are wide—the lower bound being the intrinsic value of the stock and the upper bound being the stock price itself. When we consider the no-arbitrage bounds on the sets of 10–15 option prices that are typically traded at the same time in a liquid options market, however, the bounds turn out to be much tighter. In turn, most methods will yield similar risk-neutral probability distributions, particularly in the center of the distribution, where many option prices lie. Because less information about the tails of the distributions is contained in the observed option prices, the methods tend to differ in the tails.

Empirically, this point was argued by Jackwerth and Rubinstein (1996), who decided to use five measures of the distance between the prior distribution and the risk-neutral distribution, and by Campa, Chang, and Reider, who came to a similar conclusion. They used cubic splines fitted to implied volatilities, Rubinstein's (1994) sum of the squared distance between prior and risk-neutral distributions, and mixtures of lognormal distributions. Further evidence was supplied by Coutant, Jondeau, and Rockinger (2001), who also used three methods—mixtures of lognormal distributions, HERMITE POLYNOMIAL expansions, and maximum entropy. Clews, Panigirtzoglou, and Proudman (2000) compared mixtures of two lognormals with a curve-fitting method and found much lower standard deviations of summary statistics for the curve-fitting method, which indicates that one should avoid mixtures of distributions.

In summary, because the particular choice of method does not change the results by much, an analyst might as well choose a fast and stable algorithm.

Fast and Stable Method. To deal with all of the problems described, I suggest a new method that has a number of advantages: (1) The trade-off between fit and smoothness can be controlled externally, (2) the computations are simple and can be done in an Excel spreadsheet, and (3) it requires no complicated mathematical functions or optimization routines. The formal algorithm is described in Appendix A; here, I review an example that should suffice to implement the method for any set of option prices.

Consider the following set of three option prices:

Call = 1 Put = 2	Stock Price	Strike Price	Time to Expiration	Interest Rate	Implied Volatility	Dividend Yield	Price
1	1	0.9	1	0.05	0.250	0	0.181
1	1	1.0	1	0.05	0.200	0	0.104
1	1	1.1	1	0.05	0.150	0	0.040

To keep the example manageable but still insightful, we limit ourselves to 11 future index levels that are 0.1 apart from each other, which we choose so that the strike prices (0.9, 1, and 1.1) lie within the following set:

0.5, 0.6, 0.7, 0.8, 0.9, 1, 1.1, 1.2, 1.3, 1.4, and 1.5.

If our resulting probability distribution is too coarse or does not tend to 0 in the tails, we can introduce half-steps (0.55, 0.65, etc.) or add values to the ends (0.3, 0.4, 1.6, 1.7, etc.). We discover that the trade-off parameter, λ, equal to 0.01 will provide nice results. (Normally, one needs to use trial and error here: If the distribution goes negative or is too jagged, one reduces λ; if the fitted volatilities do not match the observed volatilities sufficiently, one increases λ.)

Now, our first step is to generate a system of equations—one for each future index level—with the entries 1, –4, 6, –4, and 1 around the diagonal and –3 and 3 as the top two values of the first column and the last two values of the last column:

$$\begin{array}{llllllllllll}
3\sigma_1 & -4\sigma_2 & +1\sigma_3 & +0\sigma_4 & +0\sigma_5 & +0\sigma_6 & +0\sigma_7 & +0\sigma_8 & +0\sigma_9 & +0\sigma_{10} & +0\sigma_{11} & =0 \\
-3\sigma_1 & +6\sigma_2 & -4\sigma_3 & +1\sigma_4 & +0\sigma_5 & +0\sigma_6 & +0\sigma_7 & +0\sigma_8 & +0\sigma_9 & +0\sigma_{10} & +0\sigma_{11} & =0 \\
1\sigma_1 & -4\sigma_2 & +6\sigma_3 & -4\sigma_4 & +1\sigma_5 & +0\sigma_6 & +0\sigma_7 & +0\sigma_8 & +0\sigma_9 & +0\sigma_{10} & +0\sigma_{11} & =0 \\
0\sigma_1 & +1\sigma_2 & -4\sigma_3 & +6\sigma_4 & -4\sigma_5 & +1\sigma_6 & +0\sigma_7 & +0\sigma_8 & +0\sigma_9 & +0\sigma_{10} & +0\sigma_{11} & =0 \\
0\sigma_1 & +0\sigma_2 & +1\sigma_3 & -4\sigma_4 & +6\sigma_5 & -4\sigma_6 & +1\sigma_7 & +0\sigma_8 & +0\sigma_9 & +0\sigma_{10} & +0\sigma_{11} & =0 \\
0\sigma_1 & +0\sigma_2 & +0\sigma_3 & +1\sigma_4 & -4\sigma_5 & +6\sigma_6 & -4\sigma_7 & +1\sigma_8 & +0\sigma_9 & +0\sigma_{10} & +0\sigma_{11} & =0 \\
0\sigma_1 & +0\sigma_2 & +0\sigma_3 & +0\sigma_4 & +1\sigma_5 & -4\sigma_6 & +6\sigma_7 & -4\sigma_8 & +1\sigma_9 & +0\sigma_{10} & +0\sigma_{11} & =0 \\
0\sigma_1 & +0\sigma_2 & +0\sigma_3 & +0\sigma_4 & +0\sigma_5 & +1\sigma_6 & -4\sigma_7 & +6\sigma_8 & -4\sigma_9 & +1\sigma_{10} & +0\sigma_{11} & =0 \\
0\sigma_1 & +0\sigma_2 & +0\sigma_3 & +0\sigma_4 & +0\sigma_5 & +0\sigma_6 & +1\sigma_7 & -4\sigma_8 & +6\sigma_9 & -4\sigma_{10} & +1\sigma_{11} & =0 \\
0\sigma_1 & +0\sigma_2 & +0\sigma_3 & +0\sigma_4 & +0\sigma_5 & +0\sigma_6 & +0\sigma_7 & +1\sigma_8 & -4\sigma_9 & +6\sigma_{10} & -3\sigma_{11} & =0 \\
0\sigma_1 & +0\sigma_2 & +0\sigma_3 & +0\sigma_4 & +0\sigma_5 & +0\sigma_6 & +0\sigma_7 & +0\sigma_8 & +1\sigma_9 & -4\sigma_{10} & +3\sigma_{11} & =0
\end{array}$$

The solution of this system of equations so far is zero for each row where we multiply each coefficient with the corresponding fitted implied volatility, σ_i. But now we need to add the information concerning the observed options into the fifth, sixth, and seventh rows (corresponding to strike prices 0.9, 1, and 1.1). The required multiplier is as follows: Trade-off parameter × (Number of index levels/[Number of options × Index spacing to the fourth power]) or

$$\lambda\left[\frac{J+1}{I(\Delta^4)}\right] = 0.01\left[\frac{11}{3\times(0.1^4)}\right]$$

$$= 366.6666667.$$

We add this number to the diagonal of our system of equations for each option at Rows 5, 6, and 7. The solutions for the rows are still zero when no observed option is associated with the row, but when there is an observed option, the multiplier times the implied volatility of the observed option is used. For the three options, the result is 366.6667 multiplied by, respectively, 0.25, 0.20, and 0.15. The solutions (*Y*-variables) are then

0, 0, 0, 0, 91.6667, 73.3333, 55.0000, 0, 0, 0, and 0.

The new system of equations (with *X*-variables organized in columns so that each variable corresponds to one strike price) looks as follows:

$$
\begin{array}{llllllllllll}
3\sigma_1 & -4\sigma_2 & +1\sigma_3 & +0\sigma_4 & +0\sigma_5 & +0\sigma_6 & +0\sigma_7 & +0\sigma_8 & +0\sigma_9 & +0\sigma_{10} & +0\sigma_{11} & = 0 \\
-3\sigma_1 & +6\sigma_2 & -4\sigma_3 & +1\sigma_4 & +0\sigma_5 & +0\sigma_6 & +0\sigma_7 & +0\sigma_8 & +0\sigma_9 & +0\sigma_{10} & +0\sigma_{11} & = 0 \\
1\sigma_1 & -4\sigma_2 & +6\sigma_3 & -4\sigma_4 & +1\sigma_5 & +0\sigma_6 & +0\sigma_7 & +0\sigma_8 & +0\sigma_9 & +0\sigma_{10} & +0\sigma_{11} & = 0 \\
0\sigma_1 & +1\sigma_2 & -4\sigma_3 & +6\sigma_4 & -4\sigma_5 & +1\sigma_6 & +0\sigma_7 & +0\sigma_8 & +0\sigma_9 & +0\sigma_{10} & +0\sigma_{11} & = 0 \\
0\sigma_1 & +0\sigma_2 & +1\sigma_3 & -4\sigma_4 & +372.6667\sigma_5 & -4\sigma_6 & +1\sigma_7 & +0\sigma_8 & +0\sigma_9 & +0\sigma_{10} & +0\sigma_{11} & = 91.6667 \\
0\sigma_1 & +0\sigma_2 & +0\sigma_3 & +1\sigma_4 & -4\sigma_5 & +372.6667\sigma_6 & -4\sigma_7 & +1\sigma_8 & +0\sigma_9 & +0\sigma_{10} & +0\sigma_{11} & = 73.3333 \\
0\sigma_1 & +0\sigma_2 & +0\sigma_3 & +0\sigma_4 & +1\sigma_5 & -4\sigma_6 & +372.6667\sigma_7 & -4\sigma_8 & +1\sigma_9 & +0\sigma_{10} & +0\sigma_{11} & = 55.0000 \\
0\sigma_1 & +0\sigma_2 & +0\sigma_3 & +0\sigma_4 & +0\sigma_5 & +1\sigma_6 & -4\sigma_7 & +6\sigma_8 & -4\sigma_9 & +1\sigma_{10} & +0\sigma_{11} & = 0 \\
0\sigma_1 & +0\sigma_2 & +0\sigma_3 & +0\sigma_4 & +0\sigma_5 & +0\sigma_6 & +1\sigma_7 & -4\sigma_8 & +6\sigma_9 & -4\sigma_{10} & +1\sigma_{11} & = 0 \\
0\sigma_1 & +0\sigma_2 & +0\sigma_3 & +0\sigma_4 & +0\sigma_5 & +0\sigma_6 & +0\sigma_7 & +1\sigma_8 & -4\sigma_9 & +6\sigma_{10} & -3\sigma_{11} & = 0 \\
0\sigma_1 & +0\sigma_2 & +0\sigma_3 & +0\sigma_4 & +0\sigma_5 & +0\sigma_6 & +0\sigma_7 & +0\sigma_8 & +1\sigma_9 & -4\sigma_{10} & +3\sigma_{11} & = 0
\end{array}
$$

We now need to solve the system of equations, which can be achieved through any regression program (for example, an Excel spreadsheet): Simply regress the solution (*Y*-variable of the regression) onto the rest of the system of equations (*X*-variables of the regression, for which we use only the coefficients and suppress the σ_i). The solution is the implied volatility for each strike price equal to the future index level, and we can calculate the Black–Scholes prices associated with it, all of which information is reported in **Table 1**. As you can see, we almost perfectly matched the observed options in the market in Rows 5, 6, and 7.

The final step is to calculate the risk-neutral probabilities. We add the option prices in the rows above and below the row of the strike price we are interested in and subtract twice the option price itself. For the strike price of 0.6, this process yields

$$0.5245 + 0.3437 - 2 \times 0.4320 = 0.0041.$$

For all of the strike prices for which we can perform this calculation (0.6, . . ., 1.4), we find the following values (rounded to four decimals for greater accuracy):

0.0041, 0.0049, 0.0040, 0.0027, 0.0133, 0.0310, 0.0252, 0.0068, and 0.0005.

Table 1. Strike Prices, Implied Volatilities, Black–Scholes Prices, and Risk-Neutral Distributions

Strike Price	Implied Volatility	Black–Scholes Price	Risk-Neutral Probability
0.5	0.3165	0.5245	na
0.6	0.3132	0.4320	0.0443
0.7	0.3032	0.3437	0.0528
0.8	0.2832	0.2602	0.0432
0.9	0.2499	0.1807	0.0290
1.0	0.2000	0.1039	0.1437
1.1	0.1501	0.0403	0.3357
1.2	0.1168	0.0078	0.2722
1.3	0.0968	0.0005	0.0738
1.4	0.0868	0.0000	0.0053
1.5	0.0835	0.0000	na

na = not applicable.

Note: The risk-neutral distribution is based on Breeden and Litzenberger.

These values are not quite probabilities because they do not sum to 1, so we standardize them by dividing each by the sum of all nine values, which turns out to be 0.0925. The resulting risk-neutral probabilities are in the last column of Table 1.

We could have used a formula to obtain the risk-neutral probabilities directly from the implied volatilities to avoid having to calculate the Black–Scholes prices. This formula is provided in Appendix A, but it is so complicated that it is easier to follow the method described here.

A few final notes on implementation details may be helpful. The approach I have presented nests the Black–Scholes method, with its lognormal risk-neutral distribution, as a limiting case when trade-off parameter λ goes to zero. The higher one sets λ, the better the fit of the option prices. Thus, for this example, I tried out a few values and settled on one that yielded implied volatilities within 0.1–0.2 percent of the observed value. This choice assures, normally, that all risk-neutral probability distributions will be nonnegative and thus arbitrage free. Only a few options will be priced outside their empirical bid–ask spreads, and those tend to be options with extreme moneyness. If the risk-neutral probabilities oscillate or go negative, the analyst needs to relax the fit a little by decreasing λ.

The case of AMERICAN OPTIONS presents a problem: The methods for backing out risk-neutral distributions, including this one, strictly apply only to European option prices. To use American option prices, one has to either verify that there will be no early exercise[10] or one has to approximate the early exercise premium and subtract it from the price of the American option. One way of achieving this step is to fit a standard binomial tree (Cox, Ross, and Rubinstein) to the American option to obtain the implied volatility and then use the same binomial tree to value a hypothetical European option with the same parameters. The estimation of the risk-neutral distributions can then be based on the hypothetical European options. An alternative method is to use the approximate American option-pricing formula of Barone-Adesi and Whaley (1987) and proceed as described here. Because Cox–Ross–Rubinstein is correct in the limit, not merely an approximation, I prefer that method.

Finally, here is a real-world example of application of our methodology. I backed out the risk-neutral distributions of four international indexes corresponding to the volatility smiles of Figure 1. **Figure 5** provides the results.

The proposed method performed well. The shapes of the risk-neutral distributions are what the implied volatility smiles in Figure 1 led us to expect. Because the volatility smiles are steeply downward sloping for the United States, Germany, and the United Kingdom, we would expect the risk-neutral distributions to be left skewed and peaked in the center, just as they are in real life. The relatively flat implied volatility smile for Japan led us to suspect that the risk-neutral distribution would look more lognormal than the distribution for the other markets, and Figure 5 shows that it does.

Studies of Inverse Methods. With the risk-neutral probability distribution, one can price any arbitrary payoff with the same time to expiration. Normally, this method is applied to the pricing of exotic, illiquid options by first obtaining the risk-neutral probability distribution from plain vanilla options. This method then allows us to price the exotic options consistently with the plain vanilla options.[11]

An area of great interest is using the risk-neutral distribution to obtain tail probabilities of rare (down-market) events. Such distributions could be used, for example, in value-at-risk (VAR) applications. The work of Jackwerth and

[10]Merton gives the exact conditions when these options will not be exercised; generally, American calls that do not pay dividends should never be exercised early.

[11]Pricing American options is precluded because they lack a single time to expiration. For American options, we have to use either the approaches described in the preceding section or implied binomial trees, which are described in the section "Implied Binomial Trees." Implied binomial trees model the complete stochastic process between now at time *t* and the option expiration and are thus capable of pricing American or barrier options.

Figure 5. Risk-Neutral Implied Distributions from Options on Four International Indexes: Fast and Stable Method

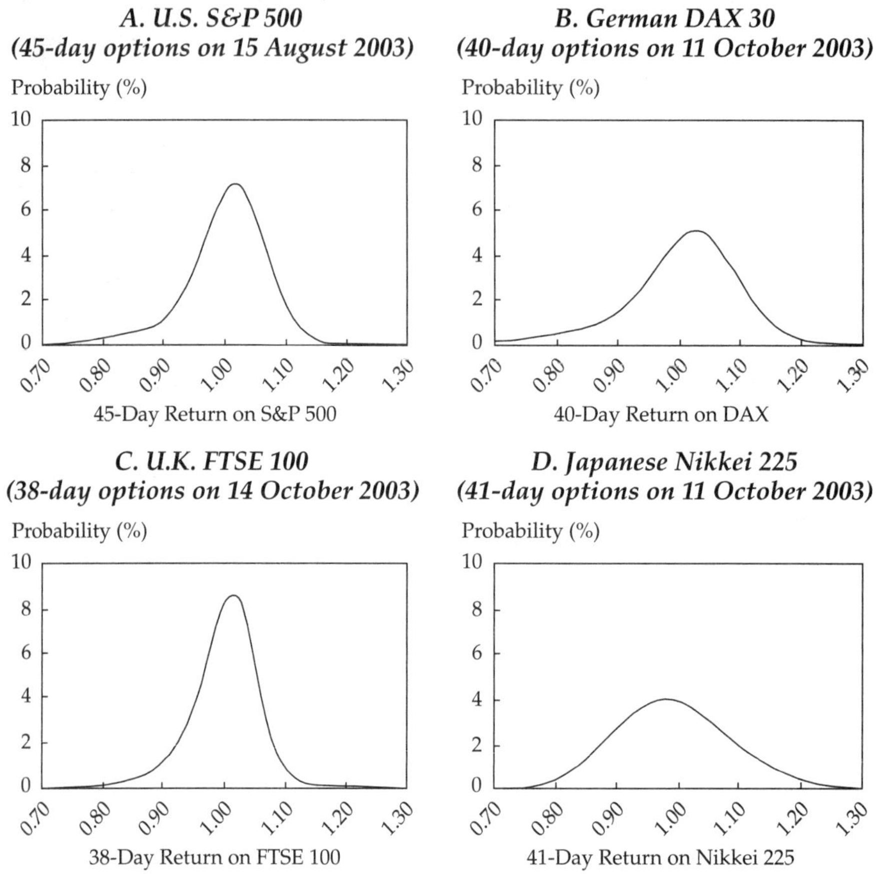

Notes: Returns reported as 1 plus the rate of return.

Rubinstein (1996) is an early example for obtaining such tail probabilities. Alas, two concerns severely limit the applicability of the method. For one, the risk-aversion adjustment will be highest for large market down moves; thus, the risk-neutral probabilities will be much higher than actual probabilities. Also, because fewer option prices are observed with very low strike prices, all methods will allocate only the correct cumulative probability to the tail but will distribute this probability arbitrarily. Thus, we cannot rely on the point estimates below the lowest observed strike price.

In trying to learn from the risk-neutral probabilities about actual probabilities, we have to remind ourselves that they will be identical only when the economy is risk neutral. That is, the utility function that holds for a risk-neutral economy is simply a linear function and investors are indifferent as to receiving a sure payment and receiving a gamble with the same expected value. Such an economy certainly does not accurately depict the world we live in.

But all is not lost yet. Rubinstein (1994) and Ziegler (2003) showed that if we are willing to assume that the economywide utility function is of standard type (say, power utility or negative exponential, as is common in academic research), the shapes of the risk-neutral distribution and the actual distribution are similar; the actual distribution simply shifts a little to the right to account for the risk premium—the difference between the mean of the actual distribution and the mean of the risk-neutral distribution (i.e., the risk-free rate). Especially for small time horizons, this difference is often small. For example, the equity risk premium for one month is only around 0.005 whereas the masses of the two distributions are concentrated in a range between –0.4 and 0.4.

Moreover, we can use the risk-neutral distribution as a good approximation of the actual distribution when the underlying security is not highly correlated with aggregate wealth—for example, orange juice. To a lesser extent, interest rates lack correlation with aggregate wealth.[12] As a result, one should consider using the tail probabilities of a risk-neutral distribution for VAR applications only if the underlying asset is little correlated with aggregate wealth (e.g., orange juice but not an index) and if one can observe prices for liquid, deep out-of-the-money puts that can be translated into call prices through put–call parity ($C = P + Sd^{-T} - Kr^{-T}$, where d is 1 plus the annualized dividend yield).

■ *Empirical studies.* Much of the empirical research on applications of risk-neutral distributions has been concerned with the impact of economic news on the shape of the risk-neutral probability distribution. A number of papers have backed out the risk-neutral probability distributions and described their changes in shape around the time of economic announcements. Campa and Chang (1996, 1998) investigated foreign exchange options in the exchange rate mechanism (ERM) and worked out the minimal and maximal risk-neutral

[12]In the section "Implied Risk Aversion," I empirically estimate the risk-neutral and actual distributions and derive the implied marginal utility.

probabilities of the exchange rate leaving the exchange rate target zone.[13] They found that option markets tend to raise the implied probabilities of leaving the target zone prior to exchange rate crises and realignments.

Bahra investigated announcements of the inflation report and of the German money supply and their impact on risk-neutral probability distributions. He suggested using the risk-neutral probability distributions to assess monetary conditions and also to identify market anomalies and investigate monetary operations.

Jondeau and Rockinger (2000) and Coutant, Jondeau, and Rockinger analyzed the French 1997 snap election and used mixtures of lognormals and Hermite polynomial expansions for, respectively, exchange rate and interest rate options. The different methods used did not change the results much. Both papers interpreted an increase in the volatility of the risk-neutral distributions as a sign that the market anticipated the result of the election.

These studies can essentially be viewed as event studies with a sample size of 1. But Brown and Jackwerth (2000) carried out a large-sample event study in which the events were macroeconomic announcements in the United States. They investigated the impact of eight announcements on the first four moments of the risk-neutral distribution of the S&P 500. The announcements were capacity utilization, the U.S. Consumer Price Index, durable goods, housing starts, industrial production, nonfarm employment, the U.S. Producer Price Index, and retail sales—announcements that spanned much of the economic activity in the United States. Particularly interesting were their findings for the second moment, which measures variance and thus the overall uncertainty in the economy, and the third moment, which measures skewness and thus the degree to which the market expects crashes to occur. Unfortunately, the main result was negative, in that the risk-neutral distributions did not seem to be affected by these macroeconomic announcements. Lynch and Panigirtzoglou (2002) asked the question in reverse, but they also found little evidence that implied volatility, skewness, or kurtosis can predict macroeconomic variables.

Steeley (2002), however, regressing the moments of the risk-neutral distribution on interest rate announcements, found some impact. Glatzer and Scheicher (2002) derived risk-neutral moments of the German DAX through a smile-fitting method and a mixture of lognormals. The higher moments differed somewhat in magnitude while being highly correlated in the two

[13]The ERM was a commitment on the part of members of the European Monetary System—most members of the European Economic Community—to maintain relatively fixed currency exchange rates. For most member currencies, fluctuations around a bilateral central rate with regard to each other currency in the European Currency Unit was to be maintained at ±2 1/4 percent from an agreed upon relationship. The ERM failed in 1992.

methods. Regressions of the implied moments on a number of macroeconomic variables did not yield relationships other than the well-known negative dependence of volatility on returns.

Instead of analyzing the whole risk-neutral distribution, the next three papers focused on the second moment, volatility, and its changes around macroeconomic announcements. Heuson and Su (2003) found that implied volatilities on interest rate options increase prior to such announcements and that this uncertainty quickly dissipates after the announcement. The movements were too small, however, to trade on profitably. Degoeij and Marquering (2002) found support for this result in the time series of actual volatilities of interest rates (as opposed to the risk-neutral dynamics underlying the implied volatilities used in the Heuson–Su study) and for the index. Beber and Brandt (2003) also investigated the second moment of the risk-neutral distribution and found, similarly, that announcements reduce the uncertainty in the U.S. Treasury interest rate market. The evidence for higher moments is less clear-cut than this evidence for volatility.

Efforts have been made to explore the determinants of the implied volatility function and thereby the risk-neutral distribution. Pena, Rubio, and Serna (1999) and Beber (2001) fitted quadratic functions to the smile and then ran regressions of the coefficients on option volume, historical volatility, volatility of volatility, and momentum. As with previous tests, the explanatory power was not high. Bollen and Whaley (2001) found that the slope of the S&P 500 smile does not explain future realized volatility, skewness, or kurtosis, but they found excess buying pressure on out-of-the money puts (e.g., because of demand for portfolio insurance) to be negatively related to the slope of the smile. Lynch and Panigirtzoglou provided a useful overview of the time-series patterns of different summary statistics of the smiles and risk-neutral distributions in several markets. Low (2000) investigated the well-known inverse relationship between returns and volatility because implied volatility reacts stronger to negative than to positive returns. He described this asymmetric relationship in terms of a reclining S-shaped function.

Because of the difficulties of obtaining and working with individual stocks' volatility smiles, most studies have investigated index smiles. A notable exception is the work of Dennis and Mayhew, who analyzed individual stock options from the CBOE. They reached six main conclusions:

- Individual stock smiles are also downward sloping but much flatter than index smiles.
- High-beta stocks and small-cap stocks have steeper smiles.
- The more actively traded stocks have steeper smiles.
- The steepness of the index smile is related to the ratio of put volume to call volume.

- The ratio of put volume to call volume has little relationship to the stock smiles.
- Contrary to standard economic arguments, the companies with more LEVERAGE tend to have flatter smiles.

Alexander (2001) applied principal component analysis to the time series of volatility smiles. Principal component analysis is a tool that separates a time series of simultaneous observations (here, implied volatilities of different strike prices) into orthogonal components. The first component is chosen to explain as much variation as possible. The second component is then chosen orthogonal to the first and chosen to explain as much of the remaining variation as possible, and so on. She concluded that the first three components (shifts, tilts, and curvature changes of the implied volatility smile) explain 80–90 percent of the variation. Principal component analysis is a purely statistical tool, however, and does not say anything about the economic causes of these moves.

What does all this research tell us? Unfortunately, not much. The implied volatility smiles of stocks and the indexes seem to move randomly around some "typical" smile. In the section "Implied Binomial Trees," we will encounter models that cover exactly such behavior (two-factor implied trees). Macroeconomic announcements seem to have little impact on the risk-neutral distributions. The only exception is that the variance of the risk-neutral distribution increases before the announcement as uncertainty increases and then decreases once the uncertainty is resolved. Leverage explains smiles to some extent, but all other explanatory variables show up only weakly if at all. Some additional studies are noted in **Exhibit 3**.[14]

▪ *Statistical tests.* A largely unresolved area of study is the development of statistical tests for risk-neutral distributions. Much of the current work lacks statistical rigor and is merely descriptive. It often simply states that graphs of risk-neutral probability distributions exhibit fatter tails or a wider spread before or after an event. A typical conclusion might read, "The distribution after the crash has a bigger left tail; thus, the market is more fearful of crashes." Some efforts are currently being made to improve the situation, however, by suggesting more rigorous ways of judging the similarity of distributions.

Söderlind and Svensson fitted a mixture of two normal distributions to the prices of bond options. They assumed normally distributed pricing errors and then estimated the multivariate normal distribution of the parameters of the mixture. They derived from this estimation the 95 percent confidence intervals of the implied risk-neutral distribution at each future bond price, which turned out to be tight.

[14]These studies are replications of research described in this section, or their results are not particularly noteworthy.

Exhibit 3. Applications of Risk-Neutral Distributions

Author (year)	Description and Notes
Andersen and Wagener (2002)	Euribor interest rate futures around 11 September 2001 attack
Bates (1991)	S&P 500 around 1987 market crash
Brenner, Eom, and Landskroner (1996)	Implied foreign exchange rate from option prices only, not whole distribution
Campa and Chang (1996, 1998)	Foreign exchange around exits from the ERM
Campa, Chang, and Refalo (1999)	Brazilian real/U.S. dollar around Brazil's 1994–99 Real Plan
Coutant, Jondeau, and Rockinger (2001)	Interest rate distributions around the French 1997 snap election
Gemmill and Saflekos (2000)	Found that option-implied risk-neutral distributions do not anticipate FTSE 100 crashes and do not show pronounced bimodalities before elections
Gereben (2002)	New Zealand dollar/U.S. dollar around the 11 September 2001 attack
Jondeau and Rockinger (2000)	French franc/German mark exchange rate around the French 1997 snap election
Leahy and Thomas (1996)	Canadian foreign exchange around the 1995 Quebec sovereignty referendum
Malz (1996)	Found estimates of realignment probabilities in the European Monetary System by using risk-reversal options
Mandler (2002)	Euribor interest rates around the European Central Bank Governing Council meetings
McCauley and Melick (1996)	Yen/U.S. dollar and German mark/U.S. dollar by using risk-reversal options
Melick and Thomas (1997)	Crude oil prices around the first Gulf War
Mizrach (1996)	British pound exchange rate around devaluation of the pound
Söderlind and Svensson (1997)	Options on bonds used to extract interest rates and inflation expectations

Söderlind (2000) started out with the fitted risk-neutral distribution, which is based on the mixtures of normal distributions. He then generated option prices that he perturbed with normally distributed errors and with bootstrapped errors (which he bootstrapped from the pricing errors generated by his initial fit of the risk-neutral distribution). He was then able to generate new risk-neutral distributions, one for each perturbed set of option prices. He found that the estimated 95 percent confidence intervals around the risk-neutral distribution change little from one simulated set of option prices to the next.

Melick and Thomas (1998), using a different dataset, conducted a study similar to Söderlind's. They found that under the strong assumption of independent and identically normally distributed pricing errors, the confidence intervals are tight. When they bootstrapped the original sample of option prices and reestimated the implied distributions, however, the resulting confidence intervals were much wider.

Bliss and Panigirtzoglou (2001) perturbed option prices within their bid–ask spreads and derived risk-neutral probability distributions based on many different perturbed sets of prices. They found that the confidence intervals around the moments of the implied distributions can be large. The resulting set of risk-neutral probability distributions is indicative of how much risk-neutral distributions can differ from each other while still being consistent with one set of option prices. Also, they found that implied distributions based on smoothed smiles perform much better than distributions based on mixtures of lognormal distributions. Cooper (1999) extended this work by using Heston's stochastic volatility model to generate the option prices rather than using market data. His results, however, closely reflect the findings in Bliss and Panigirtzoglou (2001).

Many of these studies suffered from a lack of assumptions about the error in the observed option prices. Moreover, if they did make such assumptions, we have little assurance that the pricing errors are indeed homoscedastic (that is, have the same variance at all times and for all strike prices) and independent across strike prices. A possible way out would be to use the generalized method of moments (GMM), which does not require an exact specification of the pricing errors. From a fit of such GMM estimation along the lines of Buraschi and Jackwerth's (2001) approach, one could then find confidence intervals around the parameters of the risk-neutral distribution.

Another way to assess whether two risk-neutral distributions are statistically the same is to use the Kolmogorov–Smirnov test.[15] In this case, we have to make additional assumptions, however, that the options data are being drawn from the same sample. Jiltsov (2000) developed a time series of such maximal distances of consecutive risk-neutral distributions of the FTSE 100 European options. He regressed this distance measure on option volume and open interest but could explain only 11 percent of the variation. Another avenue would be to model the evolution of the stochastic instantaneous or implied volatility surface and to base tests on these models. I discuss such models in the section "Implied Binomial Trees."

Another important issue is that the risk-neutral probability distribution is a collection of scaled prices that will not be the same as the actual probability distribution unless investors happen to be risk neutral. Some research has been concerned with the question of whether risk-neutral probability distributions are good predictors of future realized returns (see, for example, Anagnou, Bedendo, Hodges, and Tompkins 2002). The results have been largely negative, but the relationship between risk-neutral and actual probabilities is discussed further in the section "Implied Risk Aversion."

[15]The Kolmogorov–Smirnov test is explained in the section "The Actual Distribution."

In terms of the statistics of risk-neutral distributions, the conclusion is that we have not made much progress. Only when we make rather restrictive assumptions about the error structure do we obtain any encouraging results. Once we use bootstrapped errors, our confidence is much smaller. As a result, we need to be cautious in interpreting risk-neutral distributions and should refrain from reading them too literally.

Applications and Use. We are now ready to turn our attention to uses of the risk-neutral distribution for the investment professional. We can make some general observations right away.

First, any information that is drawn from the center of the distribution is quite reliable as long as we have a fair number of realistic option prices (5 is the bare minimum and, ideally, we would like more than 10).

Second, the tails beyond the last observed option are virtually useless, so any kind of VAR application should be undertaken only with restrictions in place (e.g., little correlation with aggregate wealth, good data in the tails).

Therefore, unfortunately, risk-neutral distributions, in general, do not tell us about extreme events and are of little use for most risk management applications. Their usefulness is slightly higher if we are concerned with events in the center of the distribution, such as: What is the likelihood that the return on Japanese bonds will outperform the U.S. risk-free rate? In this question, we do not have to worry about risk aversion because Japanese interest rates are not highly correlated with U.S. aggregate wealth and Japanese future interest rates are uncorrelated with the U.S. spot interest rate that is known with certainty. Also, we can use the risk-neutral distributions for relative comparisons of two securities that are highly correlated with each other and that exhibit similar risk-aversion effects (say, the S&P 500 versus Nasdaq, which we can analyze on the same moneyness scale because they are almost perfectly correlated with each other).

Another area of interest for the investment professional is using the risk-neutral distribution for making forecasts. Unfortunately, the same problems that we mentioned with respect to risk management applications are a bother in this situation. For forecasts, we need to know the actual distribution, not the risk-neutral one. The distributions will be identical only if either the economy is risk neutral (which is not likely) or if the underlying asset is uncorrelated with aggregate wealth (which can happen for certain securities—for example, weather or catastrophe derivatives). A final way to apply the risk-neutral distribution for forecasting is to be willing to assume the functional form of the utility function—say, a power utility or negative exponential utility—for the economy. Then, we know—at least for indexes, because they are highly correlated with aggregate wealth—that the actual distribution will look much like the risk-neutral distribution but is shifted to the right by the risk premium over the horizon. For short horizons, we can then use the risk-neutral distribution for making forecasts of the underlying security.

Anagnou et al. provided a survey of research that looks at whether the risk-neutral probability distribution is a good predictor of future realized stock returns. They (and most researchers) found that it is not. Bliss and Panigirtzoglou (2001), however, provide a partial list of papers that still, erroneously, interpret the risk-neutral distributions as a forecast of the future realized distribution; in essence, they assume a risk-neutral representative investor.

Rather than investigating the whole distribution, a large number of papers have examined the predictability of future realized *volatility* by historical realized volatility and option-implied volatility. Some of these works are the papers by Jorion (1995), Christensen and Prabhala (1998), Carverhill and Dyrting (2000), Fleming (1998), Blair, Poon, and Taylor (2001), and De Jong and Lehnert (2001). Unlike the results concerning the risk-neutral distribution, some evidence seems to be emerging that implied volatility rather than historical volatility is the better predictor of future volatility. Mixon (2000) investigated the predictability of future implied volatilities, as opposed to future realized volatilities, through the use of current implied volatilities. However, he did not find much forecasting ability and the forecasts were biased. Weinberg (2001) extended this analysis to the third moment but found that neither historical skewness nor option-implied skewness is a good predictor of future realized skewness.

Another application that practitioners are often interested in is how option-implied distributions can help in international finance. Comparisons of countries in terms of option-implied risk-neutral distributions will be difficult because we then need to know the correlation structure between, for example, the S&P 500 and the Japanese Nikkei 225. Rosenberg (1998, 2003) investigated this problem, but his kernel method suffers from the large amounts of data needed for the estimation. Additionally, we must be concerned that the representative investors in different countries might exhibit quite different degrees of risk aversion, which would make comparisons difficult. In particular, we cannot simply use individual preferences (say, our own); we need to use the economywide preferences, which are some kind of weighted average of all the individual ones. This aggregation is a notoriously difficult problem in economics.

The situation looks much better for applying option-implied risk-neutral distributions in portfolio management. Although portfolio managers have the same problems with risk-neutral distributions as managers in international finance, when portfolio managers need explicit forecasts, they are often more concerned with a *relative* perspective: Does the market think an appreciation in IBM is becoming more likely or less likely? In this case, the manager can use the changes in risk-neutral probabilities over a day or a week as a gauge. Because economywide preferences do not change rapidly over short periods of time, implied risk-neutral and actual distributions will be subject to a similar risk-aversion adjustment. But in that case, the portfolio manager wants to know (even though the actual probability of that event is not known) whether the increase in the risk-neutral likelihood of an event—for example, a drop in IBM by more than 5 percent—also means that the actual likelihood of this event went up by about the same amount. For asset allocation purposes, such relative information often suffices. If the manager does not believe that the market sentiment reflected in the option-implied distribution is true, then he or she might want to increase allocations to IBM. This decision would be reinforced if the manager saw the price of IBM getting depressed by the market sentiment and if IBM appeared to be a cheap buy at the time.

The main, and still the most obvious, application of the risk-neutral distribution derived from liquid vanilla options is to price illiquid securities. In this application, we found prices that are consistent with the pricing of the liquid instruments. Because we can often use the liquid options even to hedge our exposure to the exotic option, our trust in those prices is high. One shortcoming is that many exotic options are path dependent; in that case, we need to know not only the risk-neutral distribution at the terminal date but also the complete risk-neutral evolution of the underlying security through time. We will encounter such models in the section "Implied Binomial Trees."

The Actual Distribution. We have spent much time on the risk-neutral distribution, but now we need to spend some time on the issues surrounding the corresponding actual distribution over the same horizon—generally, a month or so.

Much of modern financial economics is based on the assumption of a Black–Scholes-type economy in which asset returns are lognormally distributed (that is, log returns are normally distributed). But even in the early days of finance, Mandelbrot (1963) and others noted that the distribution of daily log returns is leptokurtic; that is, the distribution exhibits fat tails and is too peaked to be normal. Also, at times, the return distribution is skewed. **Figure 6** shows such a distribution compared with a normal distribution with the same mean and variance.

Clearly, the two distributions do not match well. Two well-known reasons could be the cause. First, the return distribution may not be lognormal but leptokurtic. Second, a return distribution may be nonstationary over long periods. Returns are likely to be nonstationary if the economy fundamentally

Figure 6. Distribution of Actual Daily Log Returns against the Lognormal Distribution

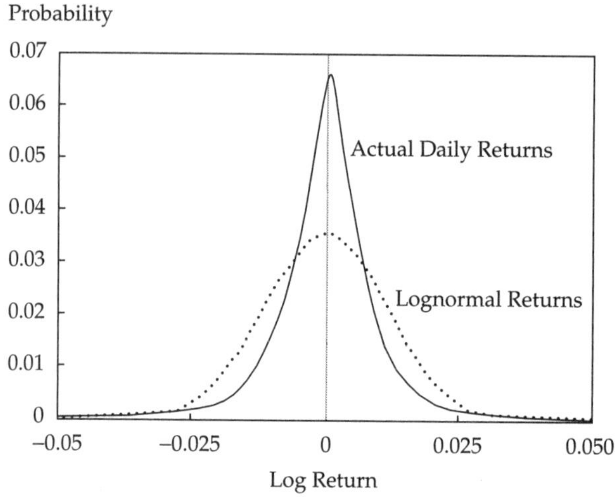

Note: Actual daily log returns on the S&P 500 for January 1928 through December 1996.

changes—as it did during the 69 years covered in Figure 6. Over the 1928–96 period, the United States went through the depression, World War II, the postwar growth, the oil crises of the early 1970s, the advent of the computer revolution, and the modern service economy. For returns from each of these periods to look systematically different from the next period's returns and for their distributions to exhibit different parameter values would not be surprising. Nonstationarity introduces leptokurtosis even if the true underlying distribution is lognormal but with time-varying parameters.

A number of researchers have criticized the lognormality assumption. For example, proponents of GARCH (generalized autoregressive conditional heteroscedasticity) models and stochastic volatility models make this point. But it might be too early to throw out the lognormality assumption for two reasons. First, in the pricing of European options, we are often concerned with horizons of one month to a year, and in portfolio theory, investment horizons tend to be even longer. Over these longer horizons, the Central Limit Theorem tends to support the lognormal model because the aggregation of daily log returns into, for example, monthly returns smooths out much of the leptokurtosis of daily returns. Second, we can sample over a shorter period so as to alleviate the nonstationarity.

In the test reported here, we sampled returns with varying horizons over sample periods of varying lengths to try to determine whether the lognormality assumption should be rejected under these conditions. This approach breaks down in the limit because we cannot calculate longer returns than the length of our sample. Nevertheless, we hope to learn from the changes in fit as we approach that limit.

To assess how well the return distribution fits the hypothesis of lognormality, we used the Kolmogorov–Smirnov test. Its main benefit is its power against any other distribution because it is a consistent test (Kendall and Stuart 1979, p. 483). The Kolmogorov–Smirnov test statistic is the maximum absolute difference between the cumulative density of the hypothesized (here, lognormal) distribution and the empirical cumulative density of the sample.

To assess the hypothesis of lognormal stock returns, we started with the full 69-year sample of daily log returns for the index and estimated the mean and variance. We then calculated the maximum difference value against the hypothesis that the true distribution is a lognormal distribution with the estimated mean and variance. At the 0.05 significance level, we compared the difference value with its critical value, and because we had to reject the hypothesis of lognormality for one-day returns, we recorded a 0 in the appropriate upper left-hand box of **Table 2**. All the other boxes were filled out in a similar fashion for sample lengths varying from one sample of 69 years to 3,312 samples of one week each. Also, we varied the returns from daily to yearly. For each subsample, we recorded a 0 for rejecting lognormality and a 1 for not rejecting it. Finally, we calculated the average of the subsamples and recorded it in the top portion of its appropriate box in Table 2. In the bottom portion of the appropriate box, we recorded the average number of returns within each subsample. The Kolmogorov–Smirnov test requires at least four observations, so we labeled boxes with fewer than six observations as "not applicable."

The results in Table 2 confirm the initial suggestions to use a comparatively short sample (months to a few years) and calculate returns with a horizon of about 1/40th of the sample length (days to weeks). The upper left-hand corner confirms the earlier results in the literature: For long samples and short return horizons, we must reject the hypothesis of lognormality. As the sample period shortens and the return horizon lengthens, however (as we move toward the center), we increasingly cannot reject lognormality. Finally, for short samples and long return horizons, we have too few observations for the Kolmogorov–Smirnov test.

The most interesting region in Table 2 is the shaded band. These combinations are all the combinations of sample lengths and return horizons for which, on average, we must reject lognormality in fewer than 20 percent of the subsamples. In 80 percent of the subsamples, we cannot reject the hypothesis of lognormality—for example, weekly returns over one year or monthly returns

Table 2. Kolmogorov–Smirnov Test-Statistics for Various Sample Sizes and Returns (average number of observations in brackets)

No. of Samples	Sample Length (years)	1-Day Returns	2-Day Returns	3-Day Returns	4-Day Returns	5-Day Returns	10-Day Returns	21-Day Returns	42-Day Returns	63-Day Returns	126-Day Returns	252-Day Returns
1	69	0	0	0	0	0	0	0	0	0	0	0
		[17,388]	[8,694]	[5,796]	[4,347]	[3,478]	[1,739]	[828]	[414]	[276]	[138]	[69]
2	30	0	0	0	0	0	0	0	0	0.5	1	1
		[7,560]	[3,780]	[2,520]	[1,890]	[1,512]	[756]	[360]	[180]	[120]	[60]	[30]
3	20	0	0	0	0.33	0	0	0	0.33	0.67	1	1
		[5,040]	[2,520]	[1,680]	[1,260]	[1,008]	[504]	[240]	[120]	[80]	[40]	[20]
6	10	0	0	0	0.33	0.17	0.17	0.33	1	0.83	0.83	1
		[2,520]	[1,260]	[840]	[630]	[504]	[252]	[120]	[60]	[40]	[20]	[10]
13	5	0	0.15	0.23	0.46	0.38	0.54	0.62	1	1	1	na
		[1,260]	[630]	[420]	[315]	[252]	[126]	[60]	[30]	[20]	[10]	[5]
34	2	0.15	0.47	0.59	0.56	0.65	0.68	0.94	0.91	0.85	na	na
		[504]	[252]	[168]	[126]	[101]	[50]	[24]	[12]	[8]	[4]	[2]
69	1	0.32	0.62	0.75	0.83	0.8	0.88	0.88	0.93	na	na	na
		[252]	[126]	[84]	[63]	[50]	[25]	[12]	[6]	[4]	[2]	[1]
138	0.5	0.57	0.78	0.87	0.91	0.88	0.89	0.85	na	na	na	na
		[126]	[63]	[42]	[32]	[25]	[13]	[6]	[3]	[2]	[1]	[1]
276	0.25	0.75	0.89	0.91	0.92	0.88	0.89	na	na	na	na	na
		[63]	[32]	[21]	[16]	[13]	[6]	[3]	[2]	[1]	[1]	[0]
828	0.08	0.9	0.91	0.92	na	na	na	na	na	na	na	na
		[21]	[11]	[7]	[5]	[4]	[2]	[1]	[1]	[0]	[0]	[0]
1,656	0.04	0.92	na	na	na	na	na	na	na	na	na	na
		[11]	[5]	[4]	[3]	[2]	[1]	[1]	[0]	[0]	[0]	[0]
3,312	0.02	na	na	na	na	na	na	na	na	na	na	na
		[5]	[3]	[2]	[1]	[1]	[1]	[0]	[0]	[0]	[0]	[0]

na = not applicable

over two years. Even for favorites of financial practitioners—such as three months of daily returns (for estimating the historical volatility for option pricing) and five years of monthly returns (for asset pricing)—we must reject lognormality for only 25 percent and 38 percent of the subsamples, respectively.

For a number of applications, the assumption of lognormally distributed returns may hold reasonably well. Often, it holds for a short sample with returns measured over a longer horizon, such as a month, for two reasons. One reason is that the sample mean is noisy so it is likely to be useless no matter how long a sample is chosen. In this case, the sample mean might be picked some other way—by, say, assuming it is the risk-free rate plus a reasonable risk premium. Second, the sample variance is somewhat insensitive to the return horizon and can reasonably be scaled up or down by the square root of time. Thus, we might be able to use a short sample with short horizon returns for the variance estimate. Even alternative variance estimates—from option-implied volatility, for example—could be used.

Implied Binomial Trees

Once we understand how to obtain risk-neutral probability distributions at a particular date, we are tempted to ask what we can infer about the stochastic process of the underlying asset that leads to this terminal distribution. In a deep and liquid options market, such as the S&P 500 options market, we can simultaneously find as many as 100 different quotes for options of different times to expiration and different strike prices. There is no unique stochastic process consistent with these option prices, however, and even if we were to know the risk-neutral probability distributions for every instant of time, there would still not be a unique stochastic process. The reason is that there could be stochastic jumps, stochastic interest rates, or stochastic volatility—any of which will give rise to multiple processes consistent with observed prices. This problem is related to the problem of market incompleteness: If we encounter too many possible states and we have too few securities and too few trading opportunities, several risk-neutral stochastic processes are feasible that will price the observed securities correctly.

Only if we are willing to limit ourselves to single-factor diffusion processes will we obtain a unique stochastic process. And implied binomial trees are simply discretizations of such generalized one-dimensional diffusion processes, in which the volatility parameter is a general function of time and the asset price. This feature sets implied binomial trees apart from the Black–Scholes formula, in which volatility is constant.[16] The drift of the implied

[16] The associated Cox–Ross–Rubinstein tree is a discretization of the Black–Scholes economy and shares this feature of exhibiting constant volatility.

binomial tree is equal to the risk-free rate when we work with risk-neutral probabilities. The pioneers of this literature are Rubinstein (1994), Derman and Kani (1994), and Dupire (1994). After describing their work, we will turn to recent extensions.

Rubinstein's Implied Binomial Trees. The simple two-step Cox–Ross–Rubinstein binomial tree serves well as an introduction to implied binomial trees. A binomial tree is a discretization of the Black–Scholes model. We assume a volatility of 0.2, a current stock price, S, of 1, and a risk-free rate of return, r, of 1.1. We further assume that no dividends are paid and that each period lasts one year. **Figure 7** exhibits the nodal stock prices and probabilities for the standard binomial tree.

We now complicate the situation by introducing a volatility smile. For every 10 percentage points of moneyness subtracted from the at-the-money option, we increase volatility by a factor of 1.1 and we do the inverse for increases in moneyness. A two-year call option with a strike price of 1.1 now has an implied volatility of 0.2/1.1 = 0.1818 and a price of 0.1497.

Figure 7. Standard Binomial Tree

A. Stock Prices

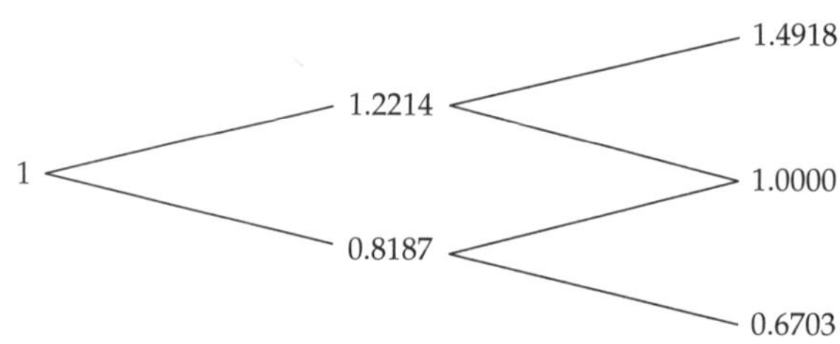

B. Nodal Probabilities

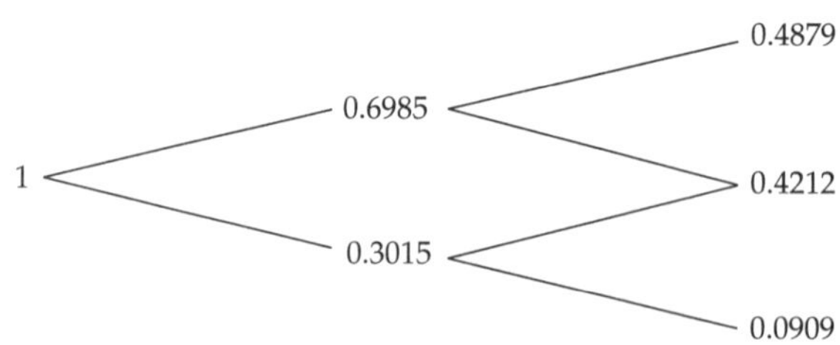

To fit a Rubinstein (1994)[17] implied binomial tree, we first need the terminal risk-neutral distribution. Given the terminal stock prices from the standard binomial tree, we now have to price the bond, the stock, and the option correctly on the basis of the risk-neutral probabilities:

$$0.8264 = \frac{1.0000P_1 + 1.0000P_2 + 1.0000P_3}{1.1^2};$$

$$1.0000 = \frac{0.6703P_1 + 1.0000P_2 + 1.4918P_3}{1.1^2};$$

$$0.1497 = \frac{0.0000P_1 + 0.0000P_2 + 0.3918P_3}{1.1^2}.$$

The resulting risk-neutral probabilities are $P_1 = 0.0527$, $P_2 = 0.4850$, and $P_3 = 0.4623$. To obtain a unique binomial tree, Rubinstein assumed that all paths that lead to the same terminal node have the same probability. That is, the center terminal probability of 0.4850 is evenly split and distributed to the two intermediate nodes. The upper intermediate node receives a total probability of 0.7048 = 0.4623 + 0.4850/2, and the process is similar for the lower intermediate node.

To work out the intermediate stock prices, we need the transition probabilities. From the upper intermediate node, the probability of moving up is 0.4623/0.7048 = 0.6559 and the probability of moving down is 0.2425/0.7048 = 0.3441. The stock price is then

$$\frac{(0.6559 \times 1.4918) + (0.3441 \times 1.0000)}{1.1} = 1.2023.$$

The stock price at the lower intermediate node can be calculated in a similar manner. The resulting implied binomial trees for the nodal stock prices and the probabilities are depicted in **Figure 8**.

Generalized Binomial Trees. Jackwerth (1997) provided an extension to the Rubinstein implied binomial tree by introducing a weight function that governs the allocation of terminal probability as one steps backward through the tree. This addition avoids the arbitrary requirement that all paths reaching the same terminal node have equal path probability and allows us to incorporate information from option prices that expire earlier than the terminal date. So, we can now also incorporate the prices of exotic and American options.

[17] All references to Rubinstein in this section are to his 1994 paper unless noted otherwise.

Figure 8. Implied Binomial Tree

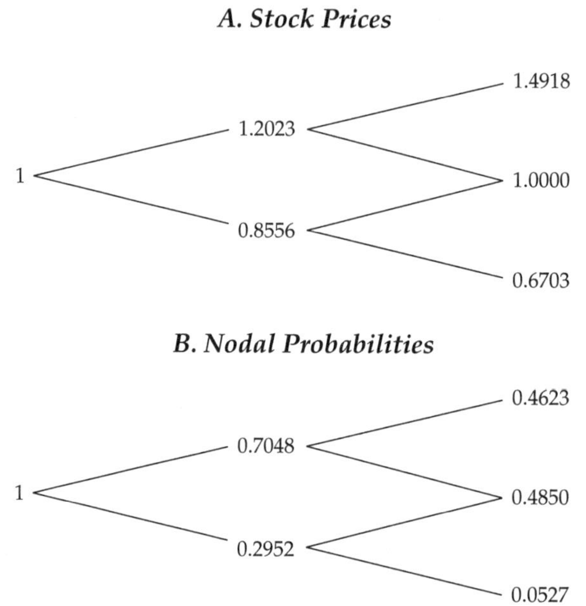

A one-year call option with strike price 1.1 would be priced on Rubinstein's implied binomial tree at

$$\frac{(0.7048 \times 0.1023) + (0.2952 \times 0.0000)}{1.1} = 0.0656,$$

but let us assume that the observed market price is 0.0724. In this case, a properly fitted generalized binomial tree can match the observed option price by splitting the center terminal probability of 0.4850, not evenly, but sending only 41.90 percent up to the intermediate upper node and sending 58.10 percent down. The upper intermediate node then receives a total probability of 0.6655 = 0.4623 + 0.2032 and the lower intermediate node is calculated similarly. We also recalculate the stock price tree in the manner described, and the resulting generalized binomial trees for the nodal stock prices and probabilities are as depicted in **Figure 9**.

Derman–Kani Trees. Derman and Kani (1994) introduced yet a different implied tree.[18] Their tree is constructed by building it up node by node by using the information in an option that expires on that particular time step and

[18]All references to Derman and Kani in this section are to their 1994 paper unless noted otherwise.

Figure 9. Generalized Binomial Tree

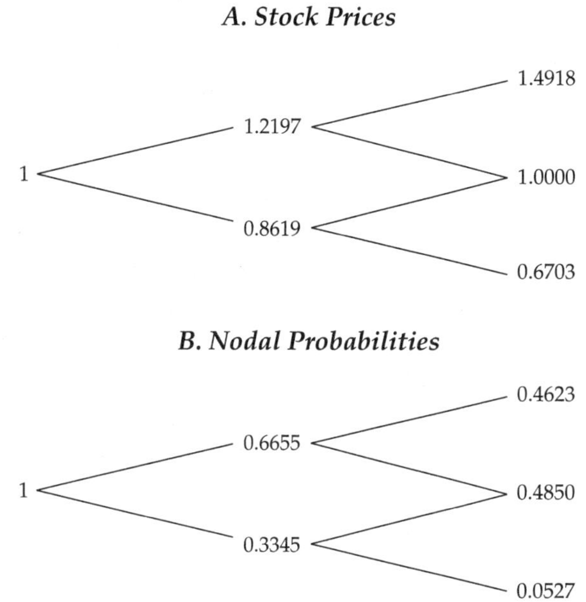

has a strike price equal to the asset price of the preceding node one step earlier. Because these exact option prices will not be observed in the market, this method requires one to interpolate and extrapolate across observed option prices.

The original Derman and Kani tree is not necessarily arbitrage free and suffers from numerical instability as the number of steps grows large. Improvements were suggested by Derman, Kani, and Chriss (1996), who introduced trinomial trees for increased stability, and by Chriss (1996), who showed how to incorporate American options through a computationally expensive optimization step.

The most important improvements, however, came from Barle and Cakici (1998), who suggested aligning the center nodes of the tree with the forward prices instead of the spot price. Furthermore, they used information from options with a strike price equal to the forward price rather than the asset price at the preceding node of the previous step. Finally, they used the Black–Scholes formula for price calculations rather than pricing options on the coarse binomial tree. A detailed example of how to calculate the Derman–Kani tree is provided in Appendix B.

Somewhat similar to the Derman and Kani tree is the Dupire tree, which is also constructed by stepping forward through the tree. It also suffers from numerical difficulties, however, and for this reason, backward-stepping trees are preferable. Cont, Da Fonseca, and Durrleman (2002) observed that the forward smile in a Derman and Kani tree cannot be time invariant. Rather, future smiles necessarily flatten out as time evolves, which is contrary to the empirical smile's behavior. A parametric tree model of interest in this context is the one developed by Guidolin and Timmermann, who modeled the stock price evolution on a tree when Bayesian learning occurs about dividend news. Their model generates symmetrical volatility smiles but not skews.

The best choice of this group seems to be the generalized binomial tree (see Jackwerth 1997) because it can incorporate information on observed exotic and American option prices. It is guaranteed to be arbitrage free, but a complete fit involves nonlinear optimization. One can avoid nonlinear optimization in the forward-stepping trees, for which I recommend using the Barle–Cakici version of the Derman–Kani tree.

Two-Factor Implied Trees. Implied binomial trees have also been extended to incorporate additional stochastic factors—stochastic volatility and stochastic implied volatility.

Derman and Kani (1998) fitted an implied trinomial tree with initially fixed transition probabilities. They then specified an exogenous stochastic process of how these transition probabilities can change. The methodology is related to the interest rate model of Heath, Jarrow, and Morton (1992), and it similarly introduces path dependence. That is, the implied tree is no longer recombining and the number of nodes explodes. Option prices can then be calculated only via MONTE CARLO SIMULATION.

Britten-Jones and Neuberger (2000) obtained the set of continuous stochastic processes that is compatible with observed option prices and that generates the same volatility forecast. They also used implied trinomial trees, for which they specified the volatility process as a discrete Markov chain. They introduced transition probabilities with which the process moves from one volatility state to the next. Although their model is more restricted than that of Derman and Kani (1998), it is also much faster to compute because it requires no Monte Carlo simulation. Neither of these models has so far been tested empirically.

Recently, a line of research has approached modeling stochastic *implied* volatilities as opposed to stochastic local volatilities. A motivation for this research is that practitioners like to work with the implied volatility surface as an *ad hoc* pricing model. Berkowitz (2001) established that this approach, when the surface is frequently updated, can provide accurate forecasts of future option prices. Dumas, Fleming, and Whaley (1998) gave credence to this argument because their deterministic volatility model performed better when implied, rather than when local, volatilities were used. Model risk, however, affects different options differently. Hull and Suo (2002) fitted a continually recalibrated deterministic volatility model to simulated European option prices written on a stochastic volatility process. They found that deterministic volatility models are better at pricing and hedging compound options than certain barrier options.

Ledoit and Santa-Clara (1998) and Amerio, Fusai, and Vulcano (2001) derived conditions under which the joint process of stock price and volatility surface is arbitrage free. Cont et al. modeled the implied volatility surface as a three-factor MEAN-REVERTING DIFFUSION, in which the factors correspond to changes in level, tilt, and curvature. (The choice of these factors was guided by the principal component analysis of the implied volatility surface in Cont and Da Fonseca 2002.) This restricted process is calibrated to observed option prices and can be used to price illiquid or exotic options via Monte Carlo simulation.

In a method similar to modeling the dynamics of the implied volatilities, Panigirtzoglou and Skiadopoulos (2002) directly modeled the evolution of the risk-neutral and cumulative risk-neutral distribution. They used principal component analysis and rotated the principal components to arrive at a two-component (two-factor) model in which the first factor is a level shift and the second factor is a change in curvature. Again, they simulated future distributions via a Monte Carlo algorithm and suggested a VAR application. Skiadopoulos and Hodges (2001) also modeled the evolution of risk-neutral mixtures of distributions when the mean or variance changes stochastically.

Other Nonparametric Models. One way to discretize the generalized volatility surface of a diffusion process is to build an implied binomial tree. This choice is particularly convenient, but alternatively, we could specify a rectangular grid in time and asset prices in which we would record the local volatilities. This alternative was proposed by Dumas, Fleming, and Whaley and is called the "deterministic volatility model." With this model, one can use finite-difference methods to price options. Andersen and Brotherson-Ratcliffe (1997) had already suggested this methodology and described various (implicit and semi-implicit) finite-difference algorithms. He argued that deterministic volatility models have computational advantages over implied binomial trees for valuing options with discontinuous payoffs, such as barrier options.

A number of authors have proposed deterministic volatility models with the additional requirement that the volatility surface be smooth. Bodurtha and Jermakyan (1996a, 1996b) and Lagnado and Osher (1997a, 1997b) are examples. But the authors all acknowledged that their algorithms are computationally expensive. Coleman, Li, and Verma (1999) found the required smooth volatility surface by using bicubic splines, which eases the computational cost.[19] Avellaneda, Friedman, Holmes, and Samperi (1997) achieved the smoothness by maximizing the cross-entropy of the fitted volatility surface and a prior surface. Their method suffers from numerical difficulties, however, because it exhibits severe spikes. Bouchouev and Isakov (1997) built up the volatility surface from rather complicated functions involving integral evaluations. They assumed that the volatility surface does not change over time, which severely restricts the flexibility of their algorithm. Brigo and Mercurio (2002) extended the mixture of distributions method to a mixture of lognormal diffusions that are all driven by the same Brownian motion. The result is a parametric volatility surface with a closed-form option-pricing formula.

Carr and Madan (2001) added more structure to the volatility surface of a deterministic volatility model by assuming that the asset price itself is path independent. This assumption implies that the asset price depends only on time and the level of the underlying diffusion process. With this additional assumption, the whole volatility surface can be obtained by observing one set of option prices with a common time to expiration. This information will normally yield only one risk-neutral probability distribution, not a complete deterministic volatility model. Carr, Tari, and Zariphopoulou (1999) described volatility surfaces that yield closed-form option-pricing formulas and gave some examples.

Laurent and Leisen (1998) added structure in a different way by restricting asset prices to lie on a prespecified grid. They modeled the transition probabilities from one node of the grid to another as a Markov chain. Their model implies an incomplete market because more states can be reached than there are available assets. Thus, they suggested either picking the risk-neutral probability distribution that yields the highest prices for all of the nontraded assets or using cross-entropy maximization to find a risk-neutral distribution that is closest to a prior distribution and still fits the observed option prices. Of these two choices, using cross-entropy maximization seems to make more economic sense; the first choice will give only an upper bound on option prices. Also investigating incomplete markets, Samperi (1996) gave bounds for option prices if the volatility surface of a deterministic volatility model is bounded between an upper and a lower bound. Assuming that investors follow risk-minimizing trading strategies, Samperi obtained a unique implied tree.

All the models described so far kept some structure for the underlying stochastic process—namely, a generalized diffusion. A final class of nonpara-

[19]"Bicubic" means order 3 in the local polynomials in both dimensions (time and asset value).

metric models, however, does away with this structure completely. Kernel methods, such as that of Aït-Sahalia and Lo (1998), view the option-pricing model as a mere exercise in interpolation and extrapolation of observed market option prices, which can be done in terms of option prices or implied volatilities. They proposed fitting a five-dimensional surface of option-implied volatilities across stock prices, strike prices, times to expiration, interest rates, and dividend yields.

Closely related in spirit are NEURAL NETWORKS, which are nonlinear regression methods with functional forms that are flexible because of the layered use of such simple functions as $f(x) = 1/(1 + e^{-x})$. These simple functions are applied to the data and then combined in weighted sums. The nodal sums of a particular layer are then used as input to the simple functions again, and weighted sums are calculated once more, yielding still fewer nodes at the second layer. After several layers, the method culminates in one single nodal value. Hutchinson, Lo, and Poggio (1994) used such a neural network on simulated Black–Scholes option prices to recover the Black–Scholes pricing formula, and they also fitted observed option prices on S&P 500 futures. Herrmann and Narr (1997) used a neural network on German index option prices.

Empirical Tests. Because of the dual difficulty of dealing with complicated option-pricing models and the paucity of large option price datasets, only two extensive studies with large samples have tested the performance of implied binomial trees. Dumas et al. approximated the volatility surface of their deterministic volatility model with polynomials in time and asset price. I will describe here a version of their model in which one fits the implied volatility surface, because this *ad hoc* extension works slightly better than the original version. For every Wednesday from June 1988 through December 1993, they fitted the volatility surface to observed prices of options on the S&P 500. One week later, they priced all options on the basis of the week-old volatility surface, where they conditioned on the change in time and asset price. These model prices were compared with market prices, and the average root mean squared prediction error was found to range from 47 cents to 59 cents for options with time to expiration of more than 70 days. The authors compared this prediction error with an average bid–ask spread of 47 cents and judged the deterministic volatility model to be generally poor.

Lim and Zhi (2002) presented findings of a more limited study of generalized binomial trees and Derman–Kani trees fitted to the British FTSE 100 options. The Derman–Kani trees come out ahead, but both models still apparently contain biases.

Fully parametric models have not fared much better. Bakshi et al. fitted parametric stochastic jump/stochastic volatility models to S&P 500 options from June 1988 through May 1991. They did not report one-week prediction errors but reported one-day prediction errors of about 40 cents for options with time to expiration of 60–180 days.

The only paper to simultaneously consider parametric methods (including a stochastic volatility model), implied binomial trees, and naive trading rules is Jackwerth and Rubinstein (1998). The naive trading rules simply assumed that the implied volatility smile in terms of strike prices (absolute model) or across moneyness (relative model) stays constant through time. The authors used options on the S&P 500 from April 1986 through December 1995 and fitted all models to daily observations of option prices. They reported the prediction errors of two-week forecasts for options with time to expiration of 135–215 days. The errors were lowest (57 cents) for the naive trading rules and similar for the implied binomial trees (75 cents) and the parametric models (78 cents). These prediction errors are noisy observations, which makes it difficult to distinguish the predictive power of the various models. Although more research into this question is certainly warranted, to dismiss implied binomial tree models at this time would be premature.

Applications and Use. Consider how an investment professional can use implied binomial trees. The applications are much more limited than in the case of the risk-neutral distributions for two reasons. First, the technology involved to set up implied binomial trees is much more complicated than the technology for obtaining a single risk-neutral distribution. And the single distribution is less sensitive to noise in the data than the same density viewed as part of a larger implied binomial tree. Second, information provided by an implied binomial tree in addition to the risk-neutral distribution is plainly overkill for most applications.

The only real reason to use implied binomial trees is to value exotic options, which depend on the complete stochastic process through time rather than simply the terminal risk-neutral distribution. For such options, the effort of calibrating an implied binomial tree to a whole range of vanilla options with different times to expiration makes sense despite the difficulties. For any other application, such as risk management, portfolio management, or forecasting, practitioners can reasonably concentrate on a particular horizon and work with the risk-neutral distribution at that date.

Implied Risk Aversion

In pricing securities, we discount the expected payoff of the security when we use risk-neutral probabilities, which will normally differ from the actual probabilities. The reason is that investors are typically risk averse. That is, promising a dollar payoff to a U.S investor in a state of the world when the investor is already wealthy is worth less to the investor than in a state where the investor is poor. The investor will, therefore, lower his or her actual probabilities to arrive at risk-neutral probabilities for pricing purposes. Similarly, the investor will raise the actual probability to arrive at a higher risk-neutral probability for dollars obtained in states of the world when he or she is poor.

In an economy in which such an investor is the representative agent and alone determines all prices, we can explicitly relate the ratio of risk-neutral probabilities, P, to actual probabilities, Q, to the scaled marginal utility, U'/ξ, which is also called the "pricing kernel," m, of the representative agent:

$$\begin{aligned} m &= \frac{U'}{\xi} \\ &= \frac{P}{r^T Q}, \end{aligned} \tag{12}$$

where ξ is the shadow price of the budget constraint. The scaling by ξ does not affect any of our results, and we will use the terms "pricing kernel" and "marginal utility" interchangeably.

Empirical Estimates of Risk Aversion and Pricing Kernels. Once we accept that the risk-neutral distribution is not the same as the actual distribution, we can try to estimate the two distributions and divide them into each other to obtain empirical functions of scaled marginal utility. Bartunek and Chowdhury (1997) were the first to do so, but they restricted the utility function to be of the power utility type. They fitted a lognormal distribution to S&P 100 Index returns and estimated risk aversion coefficients between 0.2 and 0.6 from fitting S&P 100 option prices. These values appear to be low when compared with surveys that suggest coefficients of 2–5. Bliss and Panigirtzoglou (2002) used the same parameterization and added exponential utility functions. Using data for the British FTSE 100 Index returns and options and S&P 500 returns and options, they found rather moderate risk-aversion estimates—between 2 and 7—whereas the equity premium literature suggests much higher values (e.g., 55 from Mehra and Prescott 1985). A problem with these approaches is that they parameterize the utility function rather than estimating it as a nonparametric function from the data.

A number of papers have estimated the risk-neutral distribution, however, by using one of the methods described in the section "The Inverse Problem." The authors obtained the actual distribution from fitting a time-series model to the index returns and divided the probability distributions to arrive at nonparametric empirical functions of scaled marginal utility. Using data from the S&P 500 options market, Aït-Sahalia and Lo (2000) used kernel methods for both distributions. Rosenberg and Engle fitted a curve to the implied volatility smile to obtain the risk-neutral distribution and fitted a GARCH model to the index returns. Coutant (2000) used Hermite polynomials for the risk-neutral distribution and fitted an ARCH-type model to the French CAC 40 Index. Also using the CAC 40, Perignon and Villa used kernel methods for fitting both the implied volatility smile and the historical return distribution. Hayes and Shin used a cubic spline to fit the implied volatilities across deltas in combination with a GARCH model for the S&P 500 returns. They focused on the –20 percent return event, however, and worked out the time series of marginal utility estimates for these large crashes, during which marginal utility tends to be high.

In a related method, Henrotte (2002) suggested an algorithm to obtain the pricing kernel with the smallest increase in the optimal dynamic Sharpe ratio while still pricing observed securities correctly. Chernov (2000) specified the stochastic processes that drive the economy and was then able to estimate the implied pricing kernel from time series on stocks, interest rates, and futures.

The Pricing Kernel Puzzle. Jackwerth (2000) used the implied risk-aversion functions, which are closely related to marginal utility functions (they are the negatives of the derivative of log marginal utility) and documented a so-called pricing kernel puzzle. He found that the implied marginal utility function is monotonically decreasing across wealth in a precrash period, as economic theory would suggest. That is, people grow less appreciative of additional wealth as they become wealthier. This picture changes during the postcrash period, however, when the implied marginal utility function is locally increasing in wealth for wealth levels close to the starting wealth level. The studies of Rosenberg and Engle (2002) and of Perignon and Villa confirmed these findings. Aït-Sahalia and Lo (2000) and Bliss and Panigirtzoglou (2002), however, did not find such an effect. Aït-Sahalia and Lo used a whole year of option price data and averaged the information, but these authors may have smoothed their kernel estimates too much. Bliss and Panigirtzoglou used a parametric form of the utility function, which precluded finding a potential pricing kernel puzzle *a priori*.

To provide an understanding of the pricing kernel puzzle, **Figure 10** depicts empirical estimates of the risk-neutral and the actual distributions for four international indexes. The actual distributions appear to be somewhat (log)normally distributed, whereas the risk-neutral distributions are (except for Japan) left skewed and leptokurtic; that is, they have fat left tails and are

Figure 10. Risk-Neutral and Actual Probability Distributions for Four International Indexes

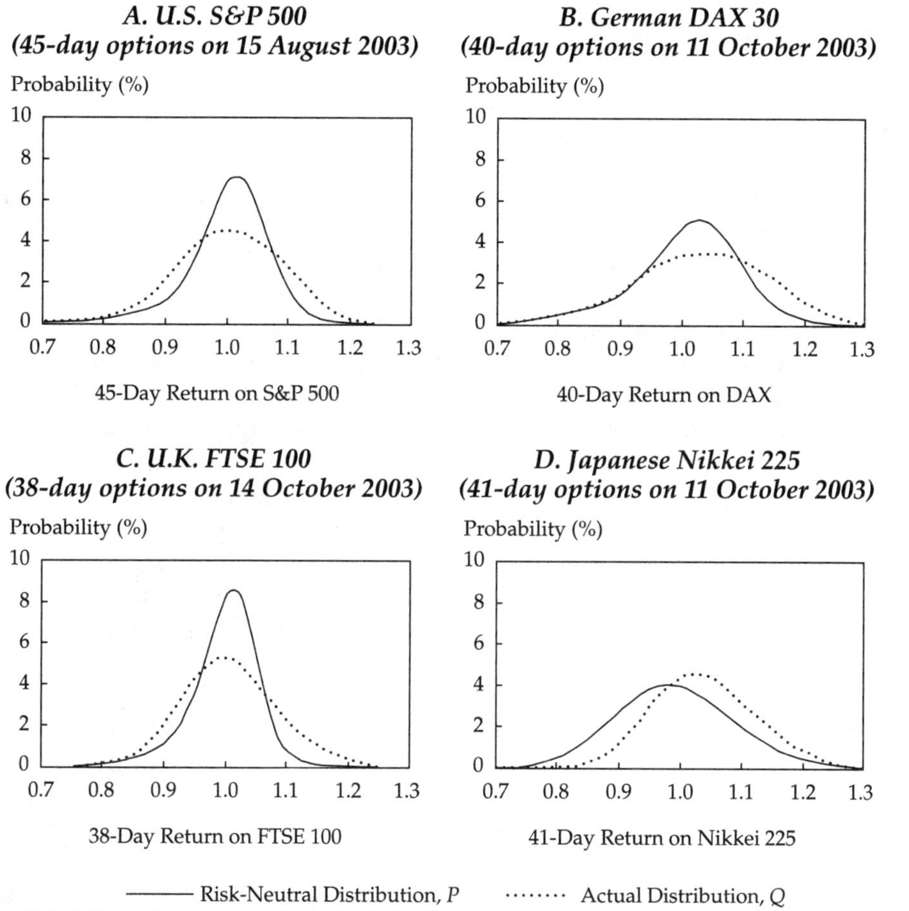

Notes: The actual distributions were calculated with the same return horizon as the time to expiration of the options. For the S&P 500, the historical sample is 2 September 1997 to 15 August 2003; for the DAX 30, the sample is 2 January 1997 to 9 October 2003; for the FTSE 100, the sample is 2 January 1997 to 9 October 2003; and for the Nikkei 225, the sample is from 5 January 1998 to 10 October 2003. Returns reported as 1 plus the rate of return. A kernel density estimator was used to generate the actual distributions. All probabilities were scaled so that the areas under the distributions would integrate to 1.

more peaked than a normal distribution. This is consistent with the underlying volatility smiles, which are depicted in Figure 1. The volatility smiles (except for Japan) are downward sloping, which prices out-of-the-money puts relatively high when compared with out-of-the-money calls. This pattern can best be viewed as "crash-o-phobia" (a term coined by Rubinstein 1994). Investors who are concerned about market crashes insure themselves by buying out-of-the-money puts, which put a floor on the maximum losses the investors can sustain. The prices of these puts are then pushed up because only a few investment banks and hedge funds are willing to supply such insurance in large quantity.

We are now ready to divide the two probability distributions into each other to obtain the empirical pricing kernels for the four international indexes, which are shown in **Figure 11**. Notice that the empirical pricing kernels are, as expected, broadly downward sloping as wealth increases. This pattern is an indication of risk-averse investors in the economy. The pricing kernel puzzle is that, theoretically, the pricing kernel should be monotonically decreasing but, at times, it increases for wealth levels close to the starting wealth level of 1. An implication of locally increasing pricing kernels is that the utility functions of the investors are locally convex. In that case, the investors would actually pay to obtain a fair gamble instead of simply pocketing the expected value of the gamble for sure. For most investors, such behavior is inconsistent with reality and contradicts our assumption that the representative investors in the different countries are risk averse. Still, the relationship that marginal utility is proportional to the ratio of risk-neutral probability and actual probability is based on this assumption. This is the puzzle, and a number of research papers have examined it.

Before we dive into possible solutions to the pricing kernel puzzle, we need to establish that it is not merely an artifact of our estimation method. Based on the dataset of daily option, bond, and index returns of Buraschi and Jackwerth, the pricing kernel puzzle can be confirmed at the daily horizon for the S&P 500. Moreover, our assumptions for the estimation are not onerous. To estimate the risk-neutral distribution, we need only assume that the observed option prices are arbitrage free. For the estimation of the actual distribution, we need to assume rational expectations. These two assumptions are commonly made in empirical work and we will do so here.

Jackwerth (2000) investigated the underlying data (on the S&P 500) and methodology in detail and did not find any problems. In particular, using various methodologies to obtain the distributions did not change the results. The results were also statistically significant: They occurred for every month in the more than eight years of data starting in June 1988 and ending in November 1995. The pricing kernel puzzle occurs in the center of the distribution and is thus not affected by mispricing of away-from-the-money options. Also, liquidity is highest around the center of the distribution, so details of market microstructure (such as bid–ask spreads, transaction costs, or margin requirements) are not likely to be causing the pricing kernel puzzle because none of those frictions changed dramatically around the crash of 1987; the pricing kernel puzzle came into existence instantaneously.

Figure 11. Empirical Pricing Kernels for Four International Indexes

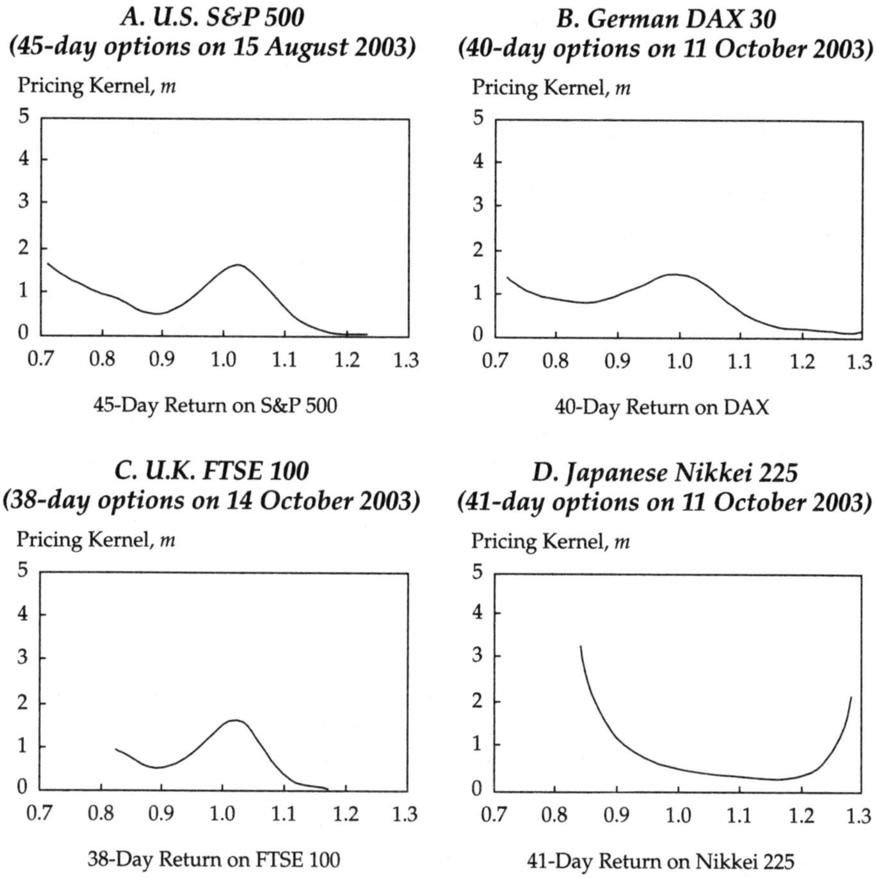

Note: The pricing kernels were calculated as the ratio of the option-implied risk-neutral distribution and the actual distribution based on historical smoothed returns.

Solutions to the Pricing Kernel Puzzle. The existing literature is largely one-sided, in that either the risk-neutral distribution or the actual distribution is being modeled; almost no work links the two aspects in terms of the pricing kernel as the scaled ratio of the two. For example (more references can be found in the section "Empirical Findings," where I discussed these works from a different perspective), the leverage effect suggests that as market values fall, the market debt-to-equity ratio (and thus index volatility) increase. As a result, we see downward-sloping implied volatility smiles, such as in Figure 1 (except for Japan). Black and others discussed the leverage effect in terms of the actual distribution; Toft and Prucyk and Dennis and Mayhew discussed it in terms of the risk-neutral distribution. None of these papers, however, connected the two aspects in terms of the pricing kernel.

The correlation effect suggests that in down markets, correlations between companies increase, so the impact of additional bad news is asymmetrical. From a different perspective, the information effect assumes that investors learn through trading, so prices can, at times, adjust sharply even without any news. Both of these effects are capable of producing a downward-sloping volatility smile, but no author has modeled the two distributions jointly.

A different line of research involves actually modeling the pricing kernel directly. This approach includes Franke, Stapleton, and Subrahmanyam (1998, 1999) with their models of background risk. Benninga and Mayshar considered heterogeneous investors, and Campbell and Cochrane (2000) modeled habit persistence—in which investors get used to their current levels of consumption and derive utility only from an increase in consumption beyond those levels. Grossman and Zhou modeled the demand and supply of portfolio insurance. But all these models have in common that their pricing kernels are monotonically decreasing in wealth, and therefore, the models do not address the pricing kernel puzzle.

Finally, a number of continuous-time models have extended the geometric Brownian motion of the Black–Scholes model. Heston's work and the GARCH model of Duan (1995), for example, introduced stochastic volatility, and Bakshi et al, Bates (2000), and Pan introduced stochastic jumps in the index and in the volatility of the index. These models move back and forth between the risk-neutral and the actual stochastic process (and their associated probability distributions) by assuming that the price of risk is proportional to the volatility or to the intensity of the jump. Alas, this particular assumption about the price of risk combined with reasonable parameter estimates leads, again, to monotonically decreasing pricing kernels. This outcome is depicted in **Figure 12** for the simulations of Pan's model, for which her estimated parameters were used.

Only a few papers have expressly dealt with the pricing kernel puzzle: Branger and Schlag (2002), Ziegler, and Brown and Jackwerth (2003).

Branger and Schlag considered an economy in which the index is composed of 30 stocks with both idiosyncratic and systematic diffusion components and also idiosyncratic and systematic jump components in their stochastic processes. (For our analysis, however, we need only concentrate on the systematic components and consider the index.) Branger and Schlag noticed that their model, by assuming that the price of jump risk is a function

Figure 12. Simulation of the Pricing Kernel in Pan

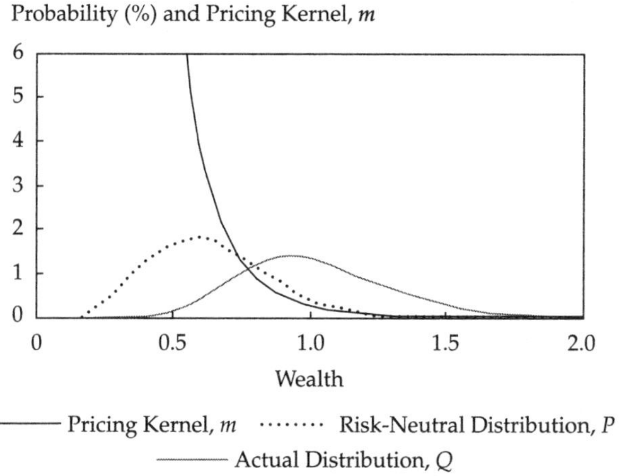

Note: Time horizon is 30 days, with 10 intradaily discrete steps in the approximation; 10,000 simulations run.

of the jump intensity, can replicate some aspects of the risk-neutral and actual distributions. When the actual distribution is being modeled with a low jump intensity, the resulting probability distribution will not look much different from a lognormal distribution and will be close to the empirical estimates. If we now assume a large price of jump risk, we will be faced with a risk-neutral probability distribution that is a mixture of the original lognormal distribution and the jump distribution. By carefully choosing the jump component, we can generate pricing kernels that are locally increasing, even if they do not show the exact shape of the empirical pricing kernel in Figure 11. Unfortunately, Branger and Schlag did not provide any economic intuition about what this pricing kernel means for the underlying economy. The pricing kernel is merely an artifact of assuming a high price of jump risk; there is no obvious equilibrium that would support such behavior in the economy.

Ziegler considered three hypotheses to explain the pricing kernel puzzle: (1) misestimation of the statistical distribution, (2) misspecification of investor preferences, and (3) heterogeneous investor beliefs. He found that errors in estimating the actual distribution would need to be oddly shaped to explain the pricing kernel puzzle. With respect to the misspecification of preferences, he argued that all the typical utility functions used in finance and economics (power utility, log utility, and negative exponential utility) yield similar transformations from the actual to the risk-neutral distribution and cannot, therefore, be the cause of the pricing kernel puzzle. Finally, he suggested that an economy with heterogeneous investors who belong to either of two about equally large groups—namely, optimists and pessimists—may explain the pricing kernel puzzle. Such investors would need to consistently believe in their distorted probability distributions, however, irrespective of the fact that the historical time series supports neither group. Rather, historical data support a more moderate probability distribution, one in the center of the two extreme views. Ziegler's model thus hinges on the fact that the heterogeneous investors do not learn from history at all.

A final contribution is the model developed by Brown and Jackwerth (2003). It considers whether a second state variable is responsible for the pricing kernel. Possible second state variables could be habit formation, recursive utility, or simply some security return, such as an interest rate or the return on any other stock. None of these variables would be able to generate the pricing kernel puzzle easily, however, because they tend to move together with aggregate wealth in a more or less linear fashion.

A more interesting candidate is volatility of the wealth process. Its potential impact on the pricing kernel is depicted in **Figure 13**. Here, the empirical pricing kernel is composed of two reference pricing kernels. The State 1 (high-volatility) pricing kernel dominates in the tails, and the State 2 (low-volatility) pricing kernel dominates in the center. As wealth increases, the likelihood of

Figure 13. Hypothetical Pricing Kernels Depending on Volatility State Variable

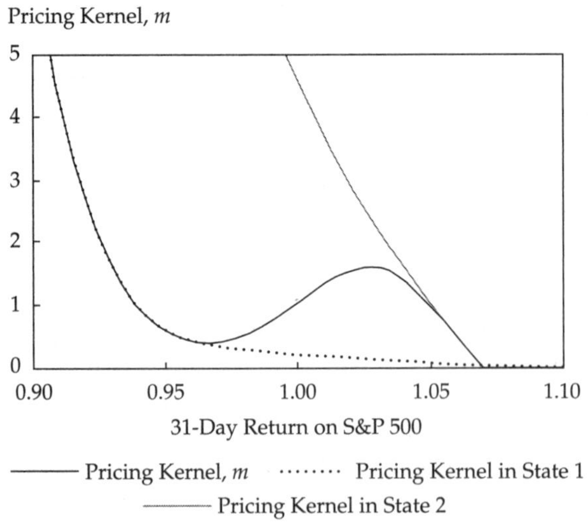

being in State 2 first increases and then decreases again. Taking the expectation over the volatility dimension yields the desired empirical pricing kernel, *m*. In combination, they can explain the pricing kernel puzzle because volatility tends to be low in the center, where aggregate wealth does not change much. If wealth either increases or decreases rapidly, however, volatility shoots up and the result is a U-shaped profile of volatility as a function of wealth. Brown and Jackwerth (2003) modeled such an economy and were indeed able to generate the pricing kernel puzzle, although it was smaller than what is shown in Figure 11. **Figure 14** shows their pricing kernel.

Figure 14. Simulated Pricing Kernel Based on Brown and Jackwerth

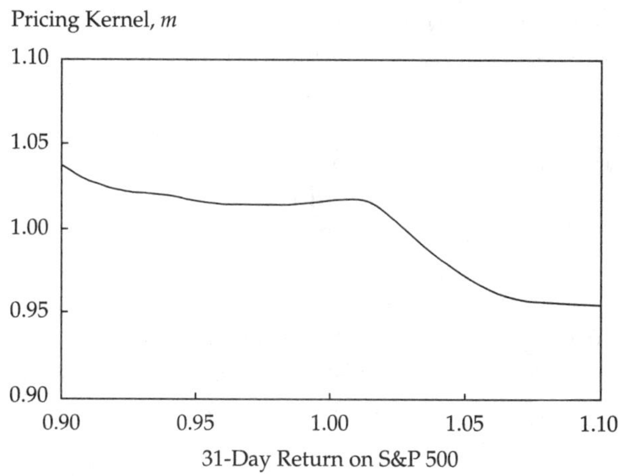

Applications and Use. The research described in this final section is certainly the least accessible in terms of using it in a practical context, but the material does have a number of applications. First, empirically plotting the pricing kernel puzzle for the index provides a measure of how much the volatility smile is out of line with option prices that are consistent with risk-averse investors. With that information, some option prices can be considered overvalued, and a gutsy trader can take advantage of that situation. This argument was made by Bondarenko (2002, 2003), Jackwerth (2000), and Jones (2001). Selling out-of-the-money puts is the most obvious strategy to make money out of overpriced portfolio insurance. This strategy entails large downside risk, however, which many traders might not want to take or cannot take because of legal restrictions (even if such trades are utility increasing).

The strategy detailed in Jackwerth (2000), however, eliminates such problems. There, the most overpriced options are found to be actually the near-the-money puts. The reason we do not see this fact in the implied volatility chart is that, although the out-of-the-money puts are the most overvalued ones in relative terms, the near-the-money puts are more overvalued in absolute terms. For a trading strategy, the absolute mispricing matters and a spread at which a trader sells the near-the-money puts and buys out-of-the-money puts (so the overall risk is comparable to being long the market) performs well. Because the out-of-the-money puts are so cheap in absolute terms, the trader is not compromising much of the profits. Although I do not know how this strategy will perform in the future, it performed well when historical data were used, with an annualized excess return of 15–25 percent.

Driessen and Maenhout (2003) confirmed these results. In their study, they used the same strategy and also investigated selling at-the-money straddles (again, protected on the downside against market crashes by the purchase of an out-of-the-money put). They found that these large profits are statistically significant and robust to corrections for transaction costs, margin requirements, and the "Peso Problem."[20] Even investors with nonexpected utility functions (those with loss aversion or disappointment aversion or those who suffer biases in decision making) would have found these trades desirable.[21] Reasons for these profitable trades could lie either in investor irrationality, when investors pay more for portfolio insurance than they should; in a negative-volatility risk premium (Bakshi and Kapadia 2003; Coval and Shumway 2001); or in a positive jump risk premium (Bates 2001; Pan).

The discussion so far has focused on index options because the index is a large part of aggregate wealth in an economy. We can, however, look at the pricing kernel across some other variable—say, interest rates. In that case, we would need to use options on bonds to find the risk-neutral distribution and we would need to sample the historical time series of interest rates to obtain the actual distribution. The pricing kernel will then be the projection of the economywide pricing kernel (which is normally defined across aggregate wealth) onto the space of interest rates. Because the correlation between interest rates and aggregate wealth is typically low, the pricing kernel at any given interest rate level will be an average of the pricing kernel levels across aggregate wealth; that is, it will be almost constant at the price of a unit discount bond.

---

[20]The Peso Problem is when a rare event (e.g., a high-interest rate regime or a market crash) occurs less frequently in the sample data than is rationally anticipated.

[21]These utility functions are described in behavioral finance and model investors who care about losses and gains with respect to a reference point (such as last period's wealth) as opposed to aggregate wealth (or consumption) or investors who consistently misestimate the probabilities of very rare or very likely events.

Empirically, we can then measure flat pricing kernels that are just below a level of 1 when the state variable is not highly correlated with aggregate wealth. A downward-sloping pricing kernel would be a sign of high positive correlation with aggregate wealth, and an upward-sloping pricing kernel would indicate state variables that can serve as a hedge because they move against movements in aggregate wealth. We could even track the time series of these pricing kernels to learn how much interest rates, for example, move together with aggregate wealth in the eyes of the market.

In conclusion, this discussion has shown that a triangular relationship exists between risk-neutral probabilities, actual probabilities, and the scaled marginal utility (pricing kernel). Given any two quantities, we can infer the third. Historically, the path taken was to assume a model for the actual probabilities and a utility function for the representative agent (or a dynamically complete market, in which case we can mathematically determine the associated pricing kernel and thereby the utility function). Then, we derived the risk-neutral probabilities and priced all the securities. Based on this section, this view has been turned upside down: We can estimate the risk-neutral and actual probability distributions to estimate the implied utility functions, which are notoriously difficult to observe.

Outlook

The crash of 1987 was a dramatic experience for the stock market. It also changed the patterns in the options markets literally from one day to the next. Whereas before the crash the implied volatility smile was largely flat and broadly consistent with Black–Scholes option prices, after the crash it became severely skewed, especially in the index option markets. As a result, much effort has been exerted to develop new parametric option-pricing models—namely, by incorporating additional stochastic factors, such as stochastic jumps, stochastic volatility, and stochastic interest rates.

A second line of research has been devoted to analyzing the observed option prices and using the implied information to price other options. The results are methods that recover the risk-neutral probability distribution from sets of option prices with common times to expiration. Once these tools became available, they were soon applied to a variety of questions in addition to pricing exotic options—for example, for investigating the impact of news on probability assessments and for forecasting. Naturally, interest has risen in learning more about the stochastic process that leads up to such terminal distribution, and implied binomial trees do provide exactly this information. Unfortunately, the world is not quite as simple as a model that we can fit to an implied volatility surface once and leave unchanged over time. Rather, the implied volatility surfaces evolve as a stochastic process, which needs to be modeled.

Risk-neutral probabilities in conjunction with actual probabilities also tell us about implied utility functions and thus about the economywide preferences that investors exhibit. This information provides a fascinating look at the economy.

Finally, I would like to speculate a bit about the future of this area of financial economics. The analysis of option-implied risk-neutral distributions is now a mature field, and it is here to stay. But questions are still open to investigation in the area of assessing the quality of these distributions, and once the effort is made to understand the cross-sectional error structure of option prices, the future will provide the necessary statistical tests. Implied binomial trees have faded in interest recently, because they are complicated to handle and cannot forecast option prices well. The other parametric option-pricing models also do not forecast option prices well, but because they are already around and being used, practitioners are showing little inclination to move to implied binomial trees. As always, the best option-pricing model will most likely turn out to be some mixed model that has parametric aspects as well as implied-tree aspects that incorporate observed market prices. The Heath–Jarrow–Morton model for interest rates might well point the way for equity option pricing.

A clear understanding of the pricing kernel puzzle will come only in time. Is it the result of widespread mispricing in the most liquid option markets across the world, or is it explainable within standard economic reasoning? The most important future developments lie in finding an improved understanding of how to move from risk-neutral to actual distributions, especially for securities that are correlated with aggregate wealth but not perfectly so. Forecasting and risk management will be much easier when research developments allow us to use the risk-neutral distributions even more than we do right now.

Appendix A. Fast and Stable Method

Theoretically, the new "fast and stable" method is related to the methods suggested in Jackwerth and Rubinstein (1996) and Jackwerth (2000). It finds a smooth risk-neutral distribution that, at the same time, explains the option prices. To implement the method, we discretize the future index value so that the spacing coincides with the strike prices:

$$S_j = S_0 + j\,\Delta, \quad \text{with } j = 0, \ldots, J, \tag{A1}$$

where

S_j = future index value

S_0 = lowest future index value evenly divisible by Δ

Δ = difference between two adjacent future index values

To find the risk-neutral probability distribution, we minimize the following objective function, for which the first-order conditions can be solved in closed form:

$$\min_{\sigma_j} \frac{\Delta^4}{2(J+1)} \sum_{j=0}^{J} \left(\sigma_j''\right)^2 + \frac{\lambda}{2I} \sum_{i=1}^{I} (\sigma_i - \bar{\sigma}_i)^2, \tag{A2}$$

where

σ_j = implied volatility associated with strike price K_j

λ = trade-off parameter for balancing smoothness versus fit

σ_j'' = second derivative of implied volatility with respect to strike prices, numerically approximated by $\sigma_j'' = (\sigma_{j-1} - 2\sigma_j + \sigma_{j+1})/\Delta^2$

σ_i = implied volatility associated with strike price K_i

$\bar{\sigma}_i$ = observed implied volatility of option with strike price K_i

The first-order conditions are for index j when there is no observed option:

$$\sigma_{j-2} - 4\sigma_{j-1} + 6\sigma_j - 4\sigma_{j+1} + \sigma_{j+2} = 0. \tag{A3}$$

For $j = 0, 1, J - 1$, and J, we set the missing implied volatilities outside the range of j to σ_0 and σ_J. When there is an observed option for index j, the first-order conditions are

$$\sigma_{j-2} - 4\sigma_{j-1} + \left[6 + \frac{\lambda(J+1)}{I\Delta^4}\right]\sigma_j - 4\sigma_{j+1} + \sigma_{j+2} = \frac{\lambda(J+1)}{I\Delta^4}\bar{\sigma}_j. \tag{A4}$$

Once we have solved the system of first-order conditions for the optimal implied volatility function, we calculate the Black–Scholes (1973) option prices across strike prices and differentiate twice with respect to the strike price. After multiplying by the risk-free return, r^T, we write down the risk-neutral probability distribution directly:

$$P(S_j) = r^T \left\{ \begin{array}{l} \dfrac{r^{-T} n(d2_j)}{S_j \sigma_j \sqrt{T}} \left(1 + 2S_j \sqrt{T} d1_j \sigma_j'\right) \\ + s d^{-T} \sqrt{T} n(d1_j) \left[\sigma_j'' + \dfrac{d1_j d2_j}{\sigma_j} (\sigma_j')^2 \right] \end{array} \right\}, \tag{A5}$$

where

$n(x)$ = standard normal density function = $\dfrac{1}{\sqrt{2\pi}} e^{-0.5x^2}$

$d1_j = \dfrac{\ln s d^{-T} / (S_j r^{-T})}{\sigma_j \sqrt{T}} + \dfrac{1}{2} \sigma_j \sqrt{T}$

$d2_j = d1_j - \sigma_j \sqrt{T}$

d = 1 + dividend yield

s = index value today

σ_j' = first derivative of implied volatility with respect to strike prices, numerically approximated by $\sigma_j' = (\sigma_{j+1} - \sigma_{j-1}) / 2\Delta$

Our approach nests the Black–Scholes economy, with its lognormal risk-neutral distribution, as a limiting case when the trade-off parameter λ goes to zero. We set the trade-off parameter empirically in such a way that we price the options accurately enough for our purposes. We reduce λ until all risk-neutral probability distributions are nonnegative—thus, arbitrage free. Only a few options tend to be priced outside their empirical bid–ask spreads, and they tend to be options with extreme moneyness.

Appendix B. Derman–Kani Implied Binomial Tree

As shown in **Figure B1**, the implied binomial tree of Derman and Kani (1994), with the corrections suggested by Barle and Cakici (1998), requires the following calculations. (I have closely followed the notation of Barle and Cakici and use all of their improvements.)

Figure B1. Derman–Kani Tree

A. Stock Prices

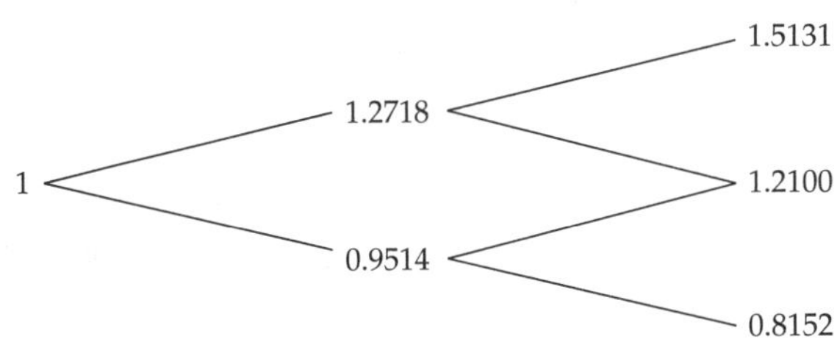

B. Nodal Probabilities

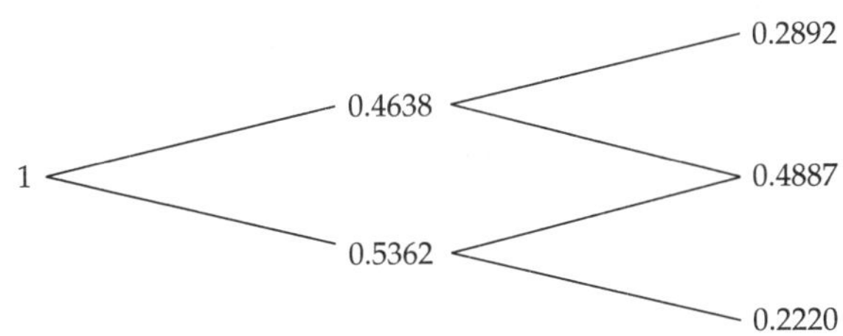

Note: With corrections of Barle and Cakici.

The lower intermediate stock price follows from (with $i = 1$):

$$\begin{aligned} S_i &= F_i \frac{\lambda_i F_i - \Delta_i^C}{\lambda_i F_i + \Delta_i^C} \\ &= 1.1 \frac{1(1.1) - 0.0797}{1(1.1) + 0.0797} \\ &= 0.9514, \end{aligned}$$

where

F_i = $S_i\,(r/d)^{\Delta t} = 1.1$
S_i = today's stock price
Δt = one time-step of one year
λ_i = the state-contingent price today (= 1)

$$\Delta_i^C = r^{\Delta t} C(F_i, t_{n+1}) - \sum_{j=i+1}^{n} \lambda_j (F_j - F_i)$$

$C(F_i, t_{n+1}) = 0.0724$ = the call expiring next period with strike price F_i

The upper intermediate stock price follows from $S_{i+1} = F_i^2 / S_i = 1.21/0.9514 = 1.2718$. The upper intermediate probability can then be derived from

$$\begin{aligned} p_i &= \frac{F_i - S_i}{S_{i+1} - S_i} \\ &= \frac{1.1 - 0.9514}{1.2718 - 0.9514} \\ &= 0.4638, \end{aligned}$$

and the lower intermediate probability is $1 - 0.4638 = 0.5362$.

To construct the terminal step, we start with the center node:

$$\begin{aligned} S_{(n/2)+1} &= S_1 \left(\frac{r}{d}\right)^{t_{n+1}} \\ &= 1.1^2 \\ &= 1.21, \end{aligned}$$

where $n = 2$.

Next, we find the upper terminal node (with $i = 2$):

$$
\begin{aligned}
S_{i+1} &= \frac{\Delta_i^C\, S_i - \lambda_i F_i (F_i - S_i)}{\Delta_i^C - \lambda_i (F_i - S_i)} \\
&= \frac{(0.03)1.21 - (0.4216)1.399(1.399 - 1.21)}{0.03 - 0.4216(1.399 - 1.21)} \\
&= 1.5131,
\end{aligned}
$$

where

F_i = $S_i(r/d)^{\Delta t} = 1.2718(1.1) = 1.399$

S_i = the stock price at the upper intermediate node

λ_i = $p_i/r^{\Delta t} = 0.4638/1.1 = 0.4216$ = the state-contingent price at the upper intermediate node

$C(F_i, t_{n+1})$ = 0.03 = the call expiring in the last period with strike price F_i

Finally, we find the lower terminal node (with $i = 1$):

$$
\begin{aligned}
S_i &= \frac{\lambda_i F_i (S_{i+1} - F_i) - \Delta_i^P S_{i+1}}{\lambda_i (S_{i+1} - F_i) - \Delta_i^P} \\
&= \frac{(0.4875)(1.0465)(1.21 - 1.0465) - (0.0467)(1.21)}{0.4875(1.21 - 1.0465) - 0.0467} \\
&= 0.8152,
\end{aligned}
$$

where

F_i = $S_i(r/d)^{\Delta t} = 0.9514(1.1) = 1.0465$

S_i = the stock price at the lower intermediate node

λ_i = $p_i/r^{\Delta t} = 0.5362/1.1 = 0.4875$ = the state-contingent price at the lower intermediate node

$$
\Delta_i^P = r^{\Delta t} P(F_i, t_{n+1}) - \sum_{j=1}^{i-1} \lambda_j (F_j - F_i)
$$

$P(F_i, t_{n+1})$ = 0.0467 = the put expiring in the last period with strike price F_i

As a last step, we calculate the transition probability between the upper intermediate node and the upper terminal node:

$$p_i = \frac{F_i - S_i}{S_{i+1} - S_i}$$

$$= \frac{1.399 - 1.21}{1.5131 - 1.21}$$

$$= 0.6236,$$

and, similarly, the transition probability between the lower intermediate node and the center terminal node:

$$p_i = \frac{F_i - S_i}{S_{i+1} - S_i}$$

$$= \frac{1.0465 - 0.8152}{1.21 - 0.8152}$$

$$= 0.5859.$$

We can now calculate the probabilities of reaching the terminal nodes. The lower node receives $0.5362(1 - 0.5859) = 0.222$, the center node receives $0.4638(1 - 0.6236) + 0.5362(0.5859) = 0.4887$, and the upper node receives $(0.4638)0.6236 = 0.2892$.

Glossary

AMERICAN OPTION: An option that can be exercised at any time on or before the expiration date.

AT-THE-MONEY CALL: A call with a strike price equal to (or very near) the market price of the underlying security.

BETA FUNCTION OF THE SECOND KIND: A generalization of the beta density function, first suggested by Bookstaber and McDonald (1987).

BID–ASK SPREAD: The difference between the current bid price (price at which an investor can sell) and the current ask price (price at which an investor can buy) for a given security.

BINOMIAL TREE: A graphical representation of a binomial model showing the possible outcomes or states associated with an option and its underlying asset. The underlying asset can only move up or down over each time step.

BROWNIAN MOTION: A continuous-time STOCHASTIC process with independent increments that have a normal distribution with mean 0 and variance 1 per unit of time.

BURR-TYPE DISTRIBUTION: A class of 12 cumulative distribution functions suggested by Burr (1942).

CALL OPTION: The right, but not the obligation, to buy a particular asset at a specified price within a specified period of time.

COMPLETE MARKET: A market in which all future payoffs on future states of the world can be constructed with existing assets.

CONFLUENT HYPERGEOMETRIC FUNCTION: A degenerate form of the hypergeometric function that arises as a solution to the confluent hypergeometric differential equation.

DELTA: See OPTION DELTA.

DIFFUSION PROCESS: A process—for example, of the logarithm of stock prices—that increases at each instant of time (drifts) and also changes randomly up or down (the diffusion term) based on a BROWNIAN MOTION.

EDGEWORTH EXPANSION: An ordering of GRAM–CHARLIER EXPANSIONS by collecting terms of equal order.

ENTROPY: A measure of distance between probabilities.

EQUITY RISK PREMIUM: The extra return that the overall stock market or a particular stock must provide over the risk-free rate to compensate for market risk.

EUROPEAN OPTION: An option that can be exercised only on the expiration date.

GEOMETRIC BROWNIAN MOTION: The process followed by a variable whose logarithm follows a BROWNIAN MOTION.

GRAM–CHARLIER EXPANSION: An approximation to the normal cumulative distribution function, using HERMITE POLYNOMIALS, in which the terms occur in sequence determined by successive derivatives of the normal density function.

HERMITE POLYNOMIALS: Successive derivatives of the normal distribution.

IMPLIED VOLATILITY: The volatility of the underlying security that causes the Black–Scholes formula to price an option exactly as observed in the market.

IN-THE-MONEY CALL: A call with a strike price below the current market price of the underlying security. (An in-the-money put is a put with a strike price above the current market price of the underlying security.)

JOHNSON FAMILY OF DENSITIES: Three different transformations of normal random variables, described by Johnson (1949) and Tadikamalla and Johnson (1982).

KERNEL METHOD: Nonparametric method for estimating the density of a random variable using so-called kernels as weighting functions.

KURTOSIS: The scaled fourth moment of a random variable governing the peakedness of the center and the fatness of the tails of the probability distribution.

LAGUERRE POLYNOMIALS: Solutions of the Laguerre differential equation.

LAMBDA DISTRIBUTION: A flexible four-parameter probability distribution used in MONTE CARLO SIMULATION, described by Corrado (2001).

LEVERAGE: The degree to which an investor or a company is using debt capital.

MEAN-REVERTING DIFFUSION: A DIFFUSION PROCESS that exhibits mean reversion—the tendency of a random process in which the greater the deviation from its mean, the greater the probability that the next measured value of the process will deviate less far. For example, in mean-reverting interest rate diffusions, very high interest rates will be followed by lower ones and very low rates will be followed by higher ones.

MONTE CARLO SIMULATION: A method for solving a problem by generating suitable random numbers and observing that fraction of the numbers that obeys some property or properties. The method is useful for obtaining numerical solutions to problems that are too complicated to solve analytically.

NEURAL NETWORK: A data-processing technique that maps, or relates, some type of input stream of information to an output stream of data. It is used, for example, to correct data with missing or distorted segments.

OPTION: The right, but not the obligation, to buy (for a call option) or sell (for a put option) a specific amount of a given stock, commodity, currency, index, or debt at a specified price (the strike price) during a specified period of time.

OPTION DELTA: The change in price of an option for every 1 percent move in the price of the underlying security. Derivative of the option price with respect to the stock price.

OUT-OF-THE-MONEY CALL: A call option whose strike price is above the current market price of the underlying security.

OUT-OF-THE-MONEY PUT: A put option whose strike price is below the current market price of the underlying security.

PRICING KERNEL: A quantity proportional to the marginal rate of substitution; ratio of STATE PRICE to actual probability. It is used for pricing securities; it lowers the probabilities of payoffs in states when the investor is already rich and vice versa. Also called the STOCHASTIC DISCOUNT FACTOR.

PUT OPTION: The right, but not the obligation, to sell a particular asset at a specified price within a specified period of time.

RISK PREMIUM: The reward for holding a risky investment rather than a risk-free one.

RISK-NEUTRAL PROBABILITIES: Probabilities that correct the actual probabilities for risk aversion.

SHARPE RATIO: A risk-adjusted measure (excess return divided by standard deviation) that is used to determine reward per unit of risk.

SKEWNESS: The scaled third moment of a random variable; it determines the asymmetry of its probability distribution.

SPLINE: A piecewise polynomial function that can have a very simple form locally but, at the same time, be globally flexible and smooth. Splines are useful for modeling arbitrary functions.

STATE PRICE: The price of a security that pays off one unit (in terms of currency or a consumption good) in only one state and zero in all other states.

STOCHASTIC: An adjective meaning random, driven by surprises or shocks.

STOCHASTIC DISCOUNT FACTOR: See PRICING KERNEL.

STRIKE PRICE: The specified price on an option contract at which the contract may be exercised. The price at which a call option buyer can buy the underlying security or a put option buyer can sell the underlying security.

VOLATILITY: The standard deviation of the return rate of an investment.

VOLATILITY SMILE: A plot of IMPLIED VOLATILITIES across option strike prices.

References

Abadir, K., and M. Rockinger. 1997. "Density-Embedding Functions." Working paper, HEC.

Abken, P., D. Madan, and S. Ramamurtie. 1996a. "Estimation of Risk-Neutral and Statistical Densities by Hermite Polynomial Approximation: With an Application to Eurodollar Futures Options." Working paper, Federal Reserve Bank of Atlanta.

———. 1996b. "Pricing S&P 500 Index Options Using a Hilbert Space Basis." Working paper, Federal Reserve Bank of Atlanta.

Aït-Sahalia, Y., and A. Lo. 1998. "Nonparametric Estimation of State-Price Densities Implicit in Financial Asset Prices." *Journal of Finance*, vol. 53, no. 2 (April):499–547.

———. 2000. "Nonparametric Risk Management and Implied Risk Aversion." *Journal of Econometrics*, vol. 94, nos. 1–2 (January/February):9–51.

Alexander, C. 2001. "Principal Component Analysis of Implied Volatility Smiles and Skews." Working paper, University of Reading.

Amerio, E., G. Fusai, and A. Vulcano. 2001. "Price of Implied Volatility Derivatives: A Risk Neutral Model for Market Implied Volatility." Working paper, INSEAD.

Anagnou, I., M. Bedendo, S. Hodges, and R. Tompkins. 2002. "The Relation between Implied and Realized Probability Density Functions." Working paper, University of Warwick.

Andersen, A., and T. Wagener. 2002. "Extracting Risk Neutral Probability Densities by Fitting Implied Volatility Smiles: Some Methodological Points and an Application to the 3M EURIBOR Futures Option Prices." Working paper, European Central Bank.

Andersen, L., and R. Brotherson-Ratcliffe. 1997. "The Equity Option Volatility Smile: An Implicit Finite Difference Approach." *Journal of Computational Finance*, vol. 1, no. 2 (Winter):5–38.

Aparicio, S., and S. Hodges. 1998. "Implied Risk-Neutral Distribution: A Comparison of Estimation Methods." Working paper, Warwick University.

Avellaneda, M., C. Friedman, R. Holmes, and D. Samperi. 1997. "Calibrating Volatility Surfaces via Relative-Entropy Minimization." *Applied Mathematical Finance*, vol. 4, no. 1 (March):37–64.

Bachelier, L. 1900. "Theorie de la Speculation," *Annales de l'Ecole Normale Superieure*, vol. 17.

Bahra, B. 1997. "Implied Risk-Neutral Probability Density Functions from Option Prices: Theory and Application." Working paper, Bank of England.

Bakshi, G., and N. Kapadia. 2003. "Delta-Hedged Gains and the Negative Market Volatility Risk Premium." *Review of Financial Studies*, vol. 16, no. 2 (Summer):527–566.

Bakshi, G., C. Cao, and Z. Chen. 1997. "Empirical Performance of Alternative Option Pricing Models." *Journal of Finance*, vol. 52, no. 5 (December):2003–49.

Banz, R., and M. Miller. 1978. "Prices for State-Contingent Claims: Some Estimates and Applications." *Journal of Business*, vol. 51, no. 4 (October):653–672.

Barle, S., and N. Cakici. 1998. "How to Grow a Smiling Tree." *Journal of Financial Engineering*, vol. 7, no. 2 (June):127–146.

Barone-Adesi, G., and R. Whaley. 1987. "Efficient Analytic Approximation of American Option Values." *Journal of Finance*, vol. 42, no. 2 (June):301–320.

Bartunek, K., and M. Chowdhury. 1997. "Implied Risk Aversion Parameters from Option Prices." *Financial Review*, vol. 32, no. 1 (February):107–124.

Bates, D. 1991. "The Crash of '87: Was It Expected? The Evidence from Options Markets." *Journal of Finance*, vol. 46, no. 3 (July):1009–44.

———. 1996. "Jumps and Stochastic Volatility: Exchange Rate Processes Implicit in Deutsche Mark Options." *Review of Financial Studies*, vol. 9, no. 1 (Spring):69–107.

———. 2000. "Post-'87 Crash Fears in S&P 500 Futures Options." *Journal of Econometrics*, vol. 94, nos. 1–2 (January/February):181–238.

———. 2001. "The Market for Crash Risk." Working Paper No. 8557, National Bureau of Economic Research, Cambridge, MA.

Beber, A. 2001. "Determinants of the Implied Volatility Function of the Italian Stock Market." Working paper, University of Pennsylvania.

Beber, A., and M. Brandt. 2003. "The Effect of Macroeconomic News on Beliefs and Preferences: Evidence from the Options Market." Working paper, St. Anna School of Advanced Studies.

Benhamou, E. 2003. "Options, Pre-Black Scholes." Working paper, Goldman Sachs.

Benninga, S., and J. Mayshar. 1997. "Heterogeneity and Option Pricing." Working paper, University of Pennsylvania.

Berkowitz, J. 2001. "Getting the Right Option Price with the Wrong Model." Working paper, University of California at Irvine.

Bernardo, A., and O. Ledoit. 2000. "Gain, Loss and Asset Pricing." *Journal of Political Economy*, vol. 108, no. 1 (February):173–206.

Black, F. 1976. "Studies of Stock Price Volatility Changes." *Proceedings of the 1976 Meetings of the American Statistical Association*, Business and Economical Statistics Section:177–181.

Black, F., and M. Scholes. 1973. "Pricing of Options and Corporate Liabilities." *Journal of Political Economy*, vol. 81, no. 3 (May/June):637–659.

Blair, B., S-H Poon, and S. Taylor. 2001. "Forecasting S&P 100 Volatility: The Incremental Information Content of Implied Volatilities and High Frequency Index Returns." *Journal of Econometrics*, vol. 105, no. 1 (November):5–26.

Bliss, R., and N. Panigirtzoglou. 2001. "Testing the Stability of Implied Probability Density Functions." *Journal of Banking and Finance*, vol. 26, no. 2–3 (March):381–422.

———. 2002. "Option-Implied Risk Aversion Estimates: Robustness and Patterns." Previously titled: "Recovering Risk Aversion from Options." Working paper, Federal Reserve Bank of Chicago.

Bodurtha, J., and M. Jermakyan. 1996a. "Non-Parametric Estimation of an Implied Volatility Surface." Working paper, Georgetown University.

———. 1996b. "Regular Smiles." Working paper, Georgetown University.

Bollen, N., and E. Rasiel. 2002. "The Performance of Alternative Valuation Models in the OTC Currency Options Market." Working paper, Vanderbilt University.

Bollen, N. and R. Whaley. 2001. "What Determines the Shape of Implied Volatility Functions?" Working paper, Vanderbilt University.

Bondarenko, O. 2000. "Recovering Risk-Neutral Densities: A New Nonparametric Approach." Working paper, University of Illinois.

———. 2002. "Why Are Puts So Expensive?" Working paper, University of Illinois.

———. 2003. "Statistical Arbitrage and Security Prices." *Review of Financial Studies*, vol. 16, no. 3 (Fall):875–919.

Boness, A. 1964. "Elements of a Theory of Stock-Option Valuation." *Journal of Political Economy*, vol. 72, no. 2 (April):163–175.

Bookstaber, R., and J. McDonald. 1987. "A General Distribution for Describing Security Price Returns." *Journal of Business*, vol. 60, no. 3 (July):401–424.

Bouchouev, I., and V. Isakov. 1997. "The Inverse Problem of Option Pricing." *Inverse Problems*, vol. 13, no. 5 (October):L11–L17.

Branger, N. 2002. "Pricing Derivative Securities using Cross-Entropy: An Economic Analysis." Working paper, School of Business and Economics, Goethe University.

Branger, N., and C. Schlag. 2002. "Why Is the Index Smile So Steep?" Working paper, University of Frankfurt.

Breeden, D., and R. Litzenberger. 1978. "Prices of State-Contingent Claims Implicit in Options Prices." *Journal of Business*, vol. 51, no. 4 (October):621–651.

Brenner, M., and Y. Eom. 1997. "No-Arbitrage Option Pricing: New Evidence on the Validity of the Martingale Property." Working paper, New York University.

Brenner, M., Y. Eom, and Y. Landskroner. 1996. "Implied Foreign Exchange Rates Using Options Prices." *International Review of Financial Analysis*, vol. 5, no. 3:171–183.

Brigo, D., and F. Mercurio. 2002. "Lognormal-Mixture Dynamics and Calibration to Volatility Smiles and Skews." *International Journal of Theoretical and Applied Finance*, vol. 5, no. 4 (June):427–446.

Britten-Jones, M., and A. Neuberger. 2000. "Option Prices, Implied Price Processes, and Stochastic Volatility." *Journal of Finance*, vol. 55, no. 2 (April):839–866.

Brown, D., and J. Jackwerth. 2000. "The Information Content of the Volatility Smile." Working paper, University of Wisconsin at Madison.

———. 2003. "The Kernel Pricing: Reconciling Index Option Data and Economic Theory." Working paper, University of Wisconsin at Madison.

Brown, G., and K. Toft. 1999. "Constructing Binomial Trees from Multiple Implied Probability Distributions." *Journal of Derivatives*, vol. 7, no. 2 (Winter):83–100.

Buchen, P., and M. Kelly. 1996. "The Maximum Entropy Distribution of an Asset Inferred from Option Prices." *Journal of Financial and Quantitative Analysis*, vol. 31, no. 1 (March):143–159.

Buraschi, A., and J. Jackwerth. 2001. "The Price of a Smile: Hedging and Spanning in Option Markets." *Review of Financial Studies*, vol. 14, no. 2 (Summer):495–527.

Burr, I. 1942. "Cumulative Frequency Functions." *Annals of Mathematical Statistics*, vol. 13:627–635.

Campa, J., and K. Chang. 1996. "Arbitrage-Based Tests of Target Zone Credibility: Evidence from ERM Cross-Rate Options." *American Economic Review*, vol. 86, no. 4 (September):726–740.

———. 1998. "ERM Realignment Risk and its Economic Determinants as Reflected in Cross-Rate Options." *Economic Journal*, vol. 108, no. 449 (July):1046–66.

Campa, J., K. Chang, and J. Refalo. 1999. "An Options-Based Analysis of Emerging Market Exchange Rate Expectations: Brazil's Real Plan, 1994–1999." Working paper, New York University.

Campa, J., K. Chang, and R. Reider. 1998. "Implied Exchange Rate Distributions: Evidence from OTC Option Markets." *Journal of International Money and Finance*, vol. 17, no. 1 (February):117–160.

Campbell, J., and J. Cochrane. 2000. "Explaining the Poor Performance of Consumption-Based Asset Pricing Models." *Journal of Finance*, vol. 55, no. 6 (December): 2863–78.

Campbell, J., and L. Hentschel. 1992. "No News Is Good News: An Asymmetric Model of Changing Volatility in Stock Returns." *Journal of Financial Economics*, vol. 31, no. 3 (June):281–318.

Campbell, R., K. Koedijk, and P. Kofman. 2002. "Increased Correlation in Bear Markets: A Downside Risk Perspective." Discussion Paper 3172, Centre for Economic Policy Research.

Carr, P., and D. Madan. 2001. "Determining Volatility Surfaces and Option Values from an Implied Volatility Smile." In *Quantitative Analysis in Financial Markets*, vol. 11. Edited by M. Avellaneda. Singapore and River Edge, NJ: World Scientific.

Carr, P., M. Tari, and T. Zariphopoulou. 1999. "Closed Form Option Valuation with Smiles." Working paper, Bank of America Securities and University of Texas at Austin.

Carverhill, A., and S. Dyrting. 2000. "The Information Content of Implied Volatility for CME Japanese Yen and S&P 500 Futures Options." Working paper, University of Science and Technology, Hong Kong.

Chernov, M. 2000. "A Case of Empirical Reverse Engineering: Estimation of the Pricing Kernel." Working paper, Pennsylvania State University.

Chriss, N. 1996. "Transatlantic Trees." *Risk*, vol. 9, no. 7 (September):46–49.

Christensen, B., and N. Prabhala. 1998. "The Relation between Implied and Realized Volatility." *Journal of Financial Economics*, vol. 50, no. 2 (November):125–150.

Christie, A. 1982. "The Stochastic Behavior of Common Stock Variance—Value, Leverage and Interest Rate Effects." *Journal of Financial Economics*, vol. 10, no. 4 (December):407–432.

Christoffersen, P., and K. Jacobs. 2001. "The Importance of the Loss Function in Option Pricing." Working paper, McGill University.

Clark, I. 2002. "Feasible Volatility Smiles and Their Implied Probability Distributions for Asset Prices." Working paper, BNP Paribas.

Clews, R., N. Panigirtzoglou, and J. Proudman. 2000. "Recent Developments in Extracting Information from Options Markets." *Bank of England Quarterly Bulletin* (February):50–60.

Cochrane, J., and J. Saa-Requejo. 2000. "Beyond Arbitrage: Good-Deal Asset Price Bounds in Incomplete Markets." *Journal of Political Economy*, vol. 108, no. 1 (February):79–119.

Coleman, T., Y. Li, and A. Verma. 1999. "Reconstructing the Unknown Volatility Function." *Journal of Computational Finance*, vol. 2, no. 3 (Spring):77–102.

Constantinides, G., and S. Perrakis. 2002. "Stochastic Dominance Bounds on Derivatives Prices in a Multiperiod Economy with Proportional Transaction Costs." *Journal of Economic Dynamics and Control*, vol. 26, no. 7–8 (July):1323–52.

Cont, R. 1997. "Beyond Implied Volatility." In *Econophysics*. Edited by J. Kertesz and I. Kondor. Dordrecht, Netherlands: Kluwer.

Cont, R., and J. da Fonseca. 2002. "Dynamics of Implied Volatility Surfaces." *Quantitative Finance*, vol. 2, no. 1 (February):45–60.

Cont, R., J. da Fonseca, and V. Durrleman. 2002. "Stochastic Models of Implied Volatility Surfaces." *Economic Notes*, vol. 31, no. 2 (July):361–377.

Cooper, N. 1999. "Testing Techniques for Estimating Implied RNDs from the Prices of European-Style Options." Working paper, Bank of England.

Corrado, C. 2001. "Option Pricing Based on the Generalized Lambda Distribution." *Journal of Futures Markets*, vol. 21, no. 3 (March):213–236.

Corrado, C., and T. Su. 1996. "Skewness and Kurtosis in S&P 500 Index Returns Implied by Option Prices." *Journal of Financial Research*, vol. 19, no. 2 (Summer): 175–192.

———. 1997. "Implied Volatility Skews and Stock Index Skewness and Kurtosis Implied by S&P 500 Index Option Prices." *Journal of Derivatives*, vol. 4, no. 4 (Summer):8–19.

Coutant, S. 2000. "Time-Varying Implied Risk Aversion in Options Prices Using Hermite Polynomials." Working paper, Banque de France.

Coutant, S., E. Jondeau, and M. Rockinger. 2001. "Reading PIBOR Futures Options' Smiles: The 1997 Snap Election." *Journal of Banking and Finance*, vol. 25, no. 11 (November): 1957–87.

Coval, J., and T. Shumway. 2001. "Expected Option Returns." *Journal of Finance*, vol. 56, no. 3 (June):983–1009.

Cox, J., S. Ross, and M. Rubinstein. 1979. "Option Pricing: A Simplified Approach." *Journal of Financial Economics*, vol. 7, no. 3 (September):229–263.

Degoeij, P., and W. Marquering. 2002. "Do Macroeconomic Announcements Cause Asymmetric Volatility?" Working paper, University of Leuven.

De Jong, C., and T. Lehnert. 2001. "Implied Garch Volatility Forecasting." Working paper, Erasmus University.

De Jong, C., and R. Huisman. 2000. "From Skews to a Skewed-*t*: Modelling Option-Implied Returns by a Skewed Student-*t*." Working paper, Erasmus University.

Dennis, P., and S. Mayhew. 2000. "Implied Volatility Smiles: Evidence from Options on Individual Equities." Working paper, University of Virginia.

Derman, E., and I. Kani. 1994. "Riding on a Smile." *Risk*, vol. 7, no. 2 (February):32–39.

———. 1998. "Stochastic Implied Trees: Arbitrage Pricing with Stochastic Term and Strike Structure of Volatility." *International Journal of Theoretical and Applied Finance*, vol. 1, no. 1 (February):61–110.

Derman, E., I. Kani, and N. Chriss. 1996. "Implied Trinomial Trees of the Volatility Smile." *Journal of Derivatives*, vol. 3, no. 4 (Summer):7–22.

Driessen, J., and P. Maenhout. 2003. "A Portfolio Perspective of Option Pricing Anomalies." Working paper, University of Amsterdam.

Duan, J. 1995. "The GARCH Option Pricing Model." *Mathematical Finance*, vol. 5, no. 1 (January):13–32.

Dumas, B., J. Fleming, and R. Whaley. 1998. "Implied Volatility Functions: Empirical Tests." *Journal of Finance*, vol. 53, no. 6 (December):2059–2106.

Dupire, B. 1994. "Pricing With a Smile." *Risk*, vol. 7, no. 1 (January):18–20.

Fleming, J. 1998. "The Quality of Market Volatility Forecasts Implied by S&P 100 Index Option Prices." *Journal of Empirical Finance*, vol. 5, no. 4 (October):317–345.

Franke, G., D. Stapleton, and M. Subrahmanyam. 1998. "Who Buys and Who Sells Options: The Role and Pricing of Options in an Economy with Background Risk." *Journal of Economic Theory*, vol. 82, no. 1 (September):89–109.

———. 1999. "When Are Options Overpriced? The Black–Scholes Model and Alternative Characterisations of the Pricing Kernel." *European Finance Review*, vol. 3, no. 1: 79–102.

French, K., G. Schwert, and R. Stambaugh. 1987. "Expected Stock Returns and Volatility." *Journal of Financial Economics*, vol. 19, no. 1 (September):3–29.

Gemmill, G., and A. Saflekos. 2000. "How Useful Are Implied Distributions? Evidence from Stock-Index Options." *Journal of Derivatives*, vol. 7, no. 3 (Spring):83–98.

Gennotte, G., and H. Leland. 1990. "Market Liquidity, Hedging, and Crashes." *American Economic Review*, vol. 80, no. 5 (December):999–1021.

Gereben, A. 2002. "Extracting Market Expectations from Option Prices: An Application to Over-the-Counter New Zealand Dollar Options." Working paper, Reserve Bank of New Zealand.

Giamouridis, D., and M. Tamvakis. 2001. "Can We Rely on Implied Distributions? Evidence from the Markets." Working paper, City University Business School.

———. 2002. "Asymptotic Distribution Expansions in Option Pricing." *Journal of Derivatives*, vol. 9, no. 4 (Summer):33–44.

Glatzer, E., and M. Scheicher. 2002. "Modelling the Implied Probability of Stock Market Declines." Working paper, Oesterreichische Nationalbank.

Grossman, S. 1988. "An Analysis of the Implications for Stock and Futures Price Volatility of Program Trading and Dynamic Hedging Strategies." *Journal of Business*, vol. 61, no. 3 (July):275–298.

Grossman, S., and Z. Zhou. 1996. "Equilibrium Analysis of Portfolio Insurance." *Journal of Finance*, vol. 51, no. 4 (September):1379–1403.

Guidolin, M., and A. Timmermann. 2000. "Option Prices and Implied Volatility Dynamics under Bayesian Learning." Working paper, University of California at San Diego.

Härdle, W. 1990. *Applied Nonparametric Regression*. Cambridge, UK: Cambridge University Press.

Härdle, W., and A. Yatchew. 2002. "Dynamic Nonparametric State Price Density Estimation Using Constrained Least Squares and the Bootstrap." Working paper, Humboldt University Berlin.

Hartvig, N., J. Jensen, and J. Pedersen. 1999. "Risk Neutral Densities of the 'Christmas Tree' Type." Working paper, Centre for Mathematical Physics and Stochastics, Aarhus University.

Hayes, S., and H. Shin. 2002. "Liquidity and Risk Appetite: Evidence from Equity Index Option Prices." Working paper, London School of Economics.

Heath, D., R. Jarrow, and A. Morton. 1992. "Bond Pricing and the Term Structure of Interest Rates: A New Methodology for Contingent Claims Valuation." *Econometrica*, vol. 60, no. 1 (January):77–105.

Henrotte, P. 2002. "Pricing Kernels and Dynamic Portfolios." Working paper, HEC.

Hentschel, L. 2003. "Errors in Implied Volatility Estimation." *Journal of Financial and Quantitative Analysis*, vol. 38, no. 4 (December):779–810.

Herrmann, R., and A. Narr. 1997. "Risk Neutrality." *Risk*, vol. 10, no. 8 (Technology Supplement):23–29.

Heston, S. 1993. "A Closed-Form Solution for Options with Stochastic Volatility with Applications to Bond and Currency Options." *Review of Financial Studies*, vol. 6, no. 2 (Summer):327–343.

Heuson, A., and T. Su. 2003. "Intra-Day Behaviour of Treasury Sector Index Option Implied Volatilities around Macroeconomic Announcements." *Financial Review*, vol. 38, no. 1 (February):161–177.

Hull, J., and W. Suo. 2002. "A Methodology for Assessing Model Risk and Its Application to the Implied Volatility Function Model." *Journal of Financial and Quantitative Analysis*, vol. 37, no. 2 (June):297–318.

Hutchinson, J., A. Lo, and T. Poggio. 1994. "A Nonparametric Approach to Pricing and Hedging Derivative Securities via Learning Networks." *Journal of Finance*, vol. 49, no. 3 (July):851–889.

Jackwerth, J. 1997. "Generalized Binomial Trees." *Journal of Derivatives*, vol. 5, no. 2 (Winter):7–17.

———. 1999. "Option Implied Risk-Neutral Distributions and Implied Binomial Trees: A Literature Review." *Journal of Derivatives*, vol. 7, no. 2 (Winter):66–82.

———. 2000. "Recovering Risk Aversion from Option Prices and Realized Returns." *Review of Financial Studies*, vol. 13, no. 2 (Summer):433–451.

Jackwerth, J., and M. Rubinstein. 1996. "Recovering Probability Distributions from Option Prices." *Journal of Finance*, vol. 51, no. 5:1611–31.

———. 1998. "Recovering Stochastic Processes from Option Prices." Working paper, University of Konstanz.

Jarrow, R., and A. Rudd. 1982. "Approximate Valuation for Arbitrary Stochastic Processes." *Journal of Financial Economics*, vol. 10, no. 3 (November):347–369.

Jarrow, R., H. Li, and F. Zhao. 2003. "Interest Rate Caps 'Smile' Too! But Can the LIBOR Market Models Capture It?" Working paper, Cornell University.

Jiltsov, A. 2000. "On the Dynamics of Option-Implied Distribution, Trading Volume and Information Arrival." Working paper, London Business School.

Johnson, N. 1949. "Systems of Frequency Curves Generated by Methods of Translation." *Biometrika*, vol. 36, no. 1–2 (June):149–176.

Jondeau, E., and M. Rockinger. 2000. "Reading the Smile: The Message Conveyed by Methods Which Infer Risk Neutral Densities." *Journal of International Money and Finance*, vol. 19, no. 6 (December):765–941.

———. 2001. "Gram-Charlier Densities." *Journal of Economic Dynamics and Control*, vol. 25, no. 10 (October):1457–83.

Jones, C. 2001. "A Nonlinear Factor Analysis of S&P 500 Index Option Returns." Working paper, University of Rochester.

Jorion, P. 1995. "Predicting Volatility in the Foreign Exchange Market." *Journal of Finance*, vol. 50, no. 2 (June):507–528.

Kelly, M. 1994. "Correlation: Stock Answer." *Risk*, vol. 7, no. 8 (August):40–43.

Kendall, M., and A. Stuart. 1979. *The Advanced Theory of Statistics*, vol. 2, 4th ed. New York: Oxford University Press.

Lagnado, R., and S. Osher. 1997a. "A Technique for Calibrating Derivative Security Pricing Models: Numerical Solution of an Inverse Problem." *Journal of Computational Finance*, vol. 1, no. 1 (Fall):13–25.

———. 1997b. "Reconciling Differences." *Risk*, vol. 10, no. 4 (April):79–83.

Laurent, J., and D. Leisen. 1998. "Building a Consistent Pricing Model from Observed Option Prices." Working paper, Hoover Institute, Stanford University.

Leahy, M., and C. Thomas. 1996. "The Sovereignty Option: The Quebec Referendum and Market Views on the Canadian Dollar." Working paper, Federal Reserve Board, Washington, DC.

Ledoit, O., and P. Santa-Clara. 1998. "Relative Pricing of Options with Stochastic Volatility." Working paper, University of California at Los Angeles.

Lim, K., and D. Zhi. 2002. "Pricing Options Using Implied Trees: Evidence from FTSE-100 Options." *Journal of Futures Markets*, vol. 22, no. 7 (July):601–626.

Longstaff, F. 1990. "Martingale Restriction Tests of Option Pricing Models." Working paper, University of California at Los Angeles.

———. 1995. "Option Pricing and the Martingale Restriction." *Review of Financial Studies*, vol. 8, no. 4 (Winter):1091–1124.

Low, C. 2000. "The Fear and Exuberance from Implied Volatility of S&P 100 Index Options." Working paper, Yale University.

Lynch, D. and N. Panigirtzoglou. 2002. "Summary Statistics of Implied Probability Density Functions and Their Properties." Working paper, Bank of England.

Malz, A. 1996. "Using Option Prices to Estimate Realignment Probabilities in the European Monetary System: The Case of Sterling–Mark." *Journal of International Money and Finance*, vol. 15, no. 5 (October):717–748.

———. 1997. "Estimating the Probability Distribution of the Future Exchange Rate from Option Prices." *Journal of Derivatives*, vol. 5, no. 2 (Winter):18–36.

Manaster, S., and G. Koehler. 1982. "The Calculation of Implied Variances from the Black–Scholes Model: A Note." *Journal of Finance*, vol. 37, no. 1 (March):227–230.

Mandelbrot, B. 1963. "The Variation of Certain Speculative Prices." *Journal of Business*, vol. 36, no. 4 (October):394–419.

Mandler, M. 2002. "Comparing Risk-Neutral Probability Density Functions Implied by Option Prices—Market Uncertainty and ECB Council Meetings." Working paper, University of Giessen.

Margrabe, B. 2002. "Option Pricing Models and Stochastic Methods in Finance, 1900–1990." Working paper, William Margrabe Group.

Masson, J., and S. Perrakis. 2000. "Option Bounds and the Pricing of the Volatility Smile," *Review of Derivatives Research*, vol. 4, no. 1 (June):29–53.

Mayhew, S. 1995. "On Estimating the Risk-Neutral Probability Distribution Implied by Option Prices." Working paper, Purdue University.

McCauley, R., and W. Melick. 1996. "Risk Reversal Risk." *Risk*, vol. 9, no. 11 (November):54–57.

Mehra, R., and E. Prescott. 1985. "The Equity Premium: A Puzzle." *Journal of Monetary Economics*, vol. 15, no. 2 (March):145–161.

Melick, W. 1999. "Results of the Estimation of Implied PDF's from a Common Dataset." Working paper, BIS Workshop.

Melick, W., and C. Thomas. 1997. "Recovering an Asset's Implied PDF from Option Prices: An Application to Crude Oil during the Gulf Crisis." *Journal of Financial and Quantitative Analysis*, vol. 32, no. 1 (March):91–115.

———. 1998. "Confidence Intervals and Constant Maturity Series for Probability Measures Extracted from Options Prices." Working paper, Kenyon College.

Merton, R. 1973. "Theory of Rational Option Pricing." *Bell Journal of Economics and Management Science*, vol. 4, no. 1 (Spring):141–183.

Mixon, S. 2000. "The Implied Volatility Term Structure of Stock Index Options." Working paper, UBS Warburg.

Mizrach, B. 1996. "Did Option Prices Predict the ERM Crisis?" Working paper, Rutgers University.

Osborne, M. 1959. "Brownian Motion in the Stock Market." *Operations Research*, vol. 7, no. 2 (March/April):145–173.

Pan, J. 2002. "The Jump-Risk Premia Implicit in Options: Evidence from an Integrated Time-Series Study." *Journal of Financial Economics*, vol. 63, no. 1 (January):3–50.

Panigirtzoglou, N., and G. Skiadopoulos. 2002. "A New Approach to Modeling the Dynamics of Implied Distributions: Theory and Evidence from the S&P 500 Options." Working paper, Bank of England.

Pena, I., G. Rubio, and G. Serna. 1999. "Why Do We Smile? On the Determinants of the Implied Volatility Function." *Journal of Banking and Finance*, vol. 23, no. 8 (August):1151–79.

Perignon, C., and C. Villa. 2002. "Extracting Information from Options Markets: Smiles, State-Price Densities and Risk Aversion." *European Financial Management*, vol. 8, no. 4 (December):495–513.

Perrakis, S. 1986. "Option Bounds in Discrete Time: Extensions and the Pricing of the American Put." *Journal of Business*, vol. 59, no. 1 (January):119–141.

Pindyck, R. 1984. "Risk, Inflation, and the Stock Market." *American Economic Review*, vol. 74, no. 3 (June):334–351.

Posner, S. and M. Milevsky. 1998. "Valuing Exotic Options by Approximating the SPD with Higher Moments." *Journal of Financial Engineering*, vol. 7, no. 2 (June):109–125.

Potters, M., R. Cont, and J. Bouchaud. 1998. "Financial Markets as Adaptive Systems." *Europhysics Letters*, vol. 41, no. 3 (February):239–244.

Pritsker, M. 1998. "Nonparametric Density Estimation and Tests of Continuous Time Interest Rate Models." *Review of Financial Studies*, vol. 11, no. 3 (Autumn):449–487.

Ritchey, R. 1990. "Call Option Valuation for Discrete Normal Mixtures." *Journal of Financial Research*, vol. 13, no. 4 (Winter):285–295.

Ritchken, P. 1985. "On Option Pricing Bounds." *Journal of Finance*, vol. 40, no. 4 (September):1219–33.

Rockinger, M., and E. Jondeau. 2002. "Entropy Densities with an Application to Autoregressive Conditional Skewness and Kurtosis." *Journal of Econometrics*, vol. 106, no. 1 (January):119–142.

Romer, D. 1993. "Rational Asset-Price Movements without News." *American Economic Review*, vol. 83, no. 5 (December):1112–30.

Rookley, C. 1997. "Fully Exploiting the Information Content of Intra Day Option Quotes: Applications in Option Pricing and Risk Management." Working paper, University of Arizona.

Rosenberg, J. 1998. "Pricing Multivariate Contingent Claims using Estimated Risk-Neutral Density Functions." *Journal of International Money and Finance*, vol. 17, no. 2 (April):229–247.

———. 2003. "Nonparametric Pricing of Multivariate Contingent Claims." *Journal of Derivatives*, vol. 10, no. 3 (Spring):9–26.

Rosenberg, J., and R. Engle. 2002. "Empirical Pricing Kernels." *Journal of Financial Economics*, vol. 64, no. 3 (June):341–372.

Ross, S. 1976. "Options and Efficiency." *Quarterly Journal of Economics*, vol. 90, no. 1 (February):75–89.

Rubinstein, M. 1985. "Nonparametric Tests of Alternative Option Pricing Models Using All Reported Trades and Quotes on the 30 Most Active CBOE Option Classes from August 23, 1976 through August 31, 1978." *Journal of Finance*, vol. 40, no. 2 (June):455–480.

———. 1994. "Implied Binomial Trees." *Journal of Finance*, vol. 49, no. 3 (July):771–818.

———. 1998. "Edgeworth Binomial Trees." *Journal of Derivatives*, vol. 5, no. 3 (Spring):20–27.

Samperi, D. 1996. "Implied Trees in Incomplete Markets." Working paper, Courant Institute, New York University.

Samuelson, P. 1965. "Rational Theory of Warrant Pricing." *Industrial Management Review*, vol. 6, no. 2 (Spring):13–31.

Schwert, G. 1989. "Why Does the Stock Market Volatility Change over Time?" *Journal of Finance*, vol. 44, no. 5 (December):1115–53.

Sharpe, W. 1964. "Capital Asset Prices: A Theory of Market Equilibrium under Conditions of Risk." *Journal of Finance*, vol. 19, no. 3 (September):425–442.

Sherrick, B., P. Garcia, and V. Tirupattur. 1995. "Recovering Probabilistic Information from Option Markets: Tests of Distributional Assumptions." Working paper, University of Illinois at Urbana-Champaign.

Sherrick, B., S. Irwin, and D. Forster. 1992. "Option-Based Evidence of the Nonstationarity of Expected S&P 500 Futures Price Distributions." *Journal of Futures Markets*, vol. 12, no. 3 (March):275–290.

———. 1996. "An Examination of Option-Implied S&P 500 Futures Price Distributions." *Financial Review*, vol. 31, no. 3 (August):667–695.

Shimko, D. 1993. "Bounds on Probability." *Risk*, vol. 6, no. 4 (April):33–37.

Silverman, B. 1986. *Density Estimation*. London: Chapman & Hall.

Skiadopoulos, G., and S. Hodges. 2001. "Simulating the Evolution of the Implied Distribution." *European Financial Management*, vol. 7, no. 4 (December):497–521.

Söderlind, P. 2000. "Market Expectations in the UK before and after the ERM Crisis." *Economica*, vol. 67, no. 265 (February):1–18.

Söderlind, P., and L. Svensson. 1997. "New Techniques to Extract Market Expectations from Financial Instruments." *Journal of Monetary Economics*, vol. 40, no. 2 (October):383–429.

Sprenkle, C. 1964. "Warrant Prices as Indicators of Expectations and Preferences." In *The Random Character of Stock Market Prices*. Edited by Paul H. Cootner. Cambridge, MA: MIT Press.

Steeley, J. 2002. "Stock Price Distribution and News: Evidence from Index Options." Working paper, University of Stirling.

Stutzer, M. 1996. "A Simple Nonparametric Approach to Derivative Security Valuation." *Journal of Finance*, vol. 51, no. 5 (December):1633–52.

Tadikamalla, P., and N. Johnson. 1982. "Systems of Frequency Curves Generated by Transformations of Logistic Variables." *Biometrika*, vol. 69, no. 2 (August):461–465.

Thorp, E., and S. Kassouf. 1967. *Beat the Market: A Scientific Stock Market System*. New York: Random House.

Toft, K., and B. Prucyk. 1997. "Options on Leveraged Equity: Theory and Empirical Tests." *Journal of Finance*, vol. 52, no. 3 (July):1151–80.

Tompkins, R. 2001. "Implied Volatility Surfaces: Uncovering the Regularities for Options on Financial Futures." *European Journal of Finance*, vol. 7, no. 3 (September): 198–230.

Weinberg, S. 2001. "Interpreting the Volatility Smile: An Examination of the Information Content of Option Price." Discussion Paper No. 706, International Finance Discussion Papers.

Young, S., G. Jabbour, M. Kramin, and T. Kramin. 2001. "Option Pricing and Higher Order Moments." Working paper, Merrill Lynch Investor Strategies Group.

Ziegler, A. 2003. "Why Does Implied Risk Aversion Smile?" Working paper, HEC.

